gray man tactics

strategies of the unseen & unknown

ISBN 9781729341551

Written in the United States of America

Table of Contents

This book is dedicated to my Mom -

Thanks for all you do!

The Modern Gray Man

There are several types of invisible people in society. These people go unnoticed by the general population because of their perceived roles and or status. The first type of people are the untouchables, those who live at the fringe of society. These people can be the homeless, impoverished, outcast, and mentally ill. The untouchables are generally limited to outside venues and are not welcome in most places of business. The second type of invisible person is the outdoor (street) worker. This includes mail carriers, construction workers, and government officials. Those wearing a reflective vest, hard hat, 2-way radio, and carrying a clipboard has surprising access in public and even private spaces. The third type of invisible person is the gray man. This type of person is most ideal when looking for a means to move about without attracting attention. The gray man isn't confined to the outdoors like the untouchables and won't need to wear a uniform as the street worker. While you can use any means to blend in when necessary, the most desirable and adaptable is the gray man.

The 21st century gray man is faced with both unique challenges and opportunities provided from a host of disciplines. With the advent of technological advancements, the means of information sharing has expanded like never before. With the integration and expansion of information systems within our societies, a change has occurred which dictates levels of individual privacy and personal freedoms. Now more than ever, one needs awareness of how technology influences quality of life, personal safety, and cultural norms.

The modern gray man is any person (male or female) who elects the path of quiet subtleness. Gray man tactics are used to move and operate in plain sight without being noticed. Skills and knowledge are needed to create opportunities to disappear from adversaries and complete specific objectives. Only a small number of people use the state of grayness, this is evident from casual observation of modern society. Most people are uninterested or oblivious to these tactics. There are personalities, characteristics, and behaviors that aid in this state of grayness. The more organic the approach the more believable and effective. There are those who struggle at being gray, some people require much effort not to be noticed. Certain people naturally contrast physically, expressively, intellectually, and or emotionally with others and environments. Not all people are the same.

For those who would struggle with gray man tactics, it's important to develop skillsets and outward demeanor. Being viewed as a hard target to criminal activity will benefit those who cannot effectively disappear within society. Use known gray man tactics when possible, but continue to refine capabilities to give options when needed. Criminals prey on the feeble, they also target the gray man when perceived as weak. But even the best hard targets are vulnerable – we all have weaknesses. Ultimately, gray man tactics are tools for evading, moving, and operating in plain sight. This is not something you would use in everyday life, but something of valuable when needed.

In this book, the gray man concept will be discussed with details and examples. Insights on gray man philosophy is not easily found, thus it's the authors attempt in this overview to pull together relevant information. No book can be a substitute for all encountered situations, but a foundation can be constructed within the concept of gray man awareness. Awareness is the cornerstone for effective management of social behavior. How you act influences how others perceive and act towards you and others. Learning what motivates and pleases others allows for enhanced manipulations within your environment. The more you know of your surroundings the more you can influence it.

The modern gray man is open minded and aware, keen and realistic. Confident in self, the gray man uses knowledge and skills to create or influence what is needed to thrive. They understand their world to know their place within it. The gray man experiences personal growth from awareness and connection. They challenge societal concepts and mainstream rhetoric, they know the difference between truth and deceit. They understand that beliefs influence the world around them, this in turn creates a reality. They know to protect from disinformation and unwarranted distractions. Fear and panic is an actuality in today's world, but the gray man stays calm and rational.

Gray Man Objectives

"Watch your thoughts; they become words. Watch your words; they become actions. Watch your actions; they become habits. Watch your habits; they become character. Watch your character; it becomes your destiny." – Frank Outlaw

The core gray man objective is blending in with the environment - to flow with society. Contrast is eliminated and seamless continuity with others becomes a nature state of being. The gray man isn't memorable, they pass through as ordinary - as boring. The gray man does what others are doing, they look where others look, say what others say, and move with the group. They avoid tracking and recording technology when in public and private spaces. The gray man is aware of resources in their environment.

Peaceful and beneficial social interactions lead to pleasant relationships. Effective problem solving eliminates drama and attention when done in a direct and humble manner. While social interactions may be necessary in public spaces, minimize them when possible. Objectives include not being remembered, noticed, and talked about. Appear to be uninteresting or routine, it's hard to remember something that creates no stimulus.

When moving through your day avoid distracting other people, blend in like a chameleon. Look for ways to move about in your routine without looking like you are avoiding attention. Make calculated covert behavior look natural and ordinary. Play along with unexpected situations and be adaptable to problems. Don't look at the world as a paranoid person would, but see the underlining nature of everyday threats. See how things can be used against you and counter them with stealth and confidence.

Looking calm and settled increases the probability of accessing restricted locations without suspicion. People accept those who appear to belong. Clandestine operatives use this technique to act their way into controlled environments. Look the part, be confident, project authority when needed and humility otherwise. Merge with social norms and don't question the environmental flow. Those who accept their surroundings appear to the most natural in them. Play the part not with logic but with heart. Feel your way through situations with intuition and gut instinct.

Gray Man S.O.P.

"If A equals success, then the formula is: A=X+Y+Z. X is work. Y is play. Z is keep your mouth shut." – Albert Einstein

The gray man S.O.P. (standard operating procedure) is deceivingly simple yet effective. Use the core objective to reinforce the procedures. The S.O.P. begins with identification of social norms, this is your baseline in which to build from. Within the social norms find the flow in which things happen, there's a rhythm in all environments. Connect with this rhythm by integrating with the surroundings, be a part of it.

Use OPSEC (operational security) to deduce what information should be publicly shared. If information can be used against you then it should be withheld from public sources. This includes conversations in communal spaces, social media interactions, and any other compromising scenarios where explicit information could yield a threat to safety and wellbeing. Identity theft is one example of why one would protect private information.

OPSEC includes not only controlling the outflow of sensitive information but also how you regulate your schedule. Schedules should be varied as much as possible, behavior should not be easily predictable. Mix up your schedule when possible, it makes life more exciting and keeps those tracking you on edge. Make yourself a hard target from criminals, be someone not desirable to deal with in a self-defense scenario. This is not to say that you shouldn't be polite to others, just be simple in your courtesy – be forgettable.

Your personal security has much to do with how much information you give to others and how much they have access to your daily routines. By changing how you conceal personal information you can limit damage done to you and your family. Some things like locking doors, keeping passwords on computer files, and using backup encrypted drives are sure ways to protect yourself. While you don't want to go through life looking over your shoulder, you do want to have a reasonable level of privacy. We all need a defense against those who desire to do harm.

It's advisable to simplify your life to maximize flexibility. A simple lifestyle affords more opportunity to adapt than one with rigid schedules and demanding responsibilities. We all have responsibilities, but to overburden ourselves benefits no one and attracts others with mal intent. The more we are distracted the more others can take advantage of us.

Use conscious awareness throughout the day to yield solutions to presented challenges. Better choices come from having a pool of options to draw from. Some solutions will prove more useful than others, but having choices will increase your chance of making a more efficient one. Problem solving with the use of awareness is a foundational skill and activity the gray man continuously exercises. Look at problems from different perspectives, this may include sourcing information from others and doing additional research.

When in public notice those who seem the most ordinary. Study what makes them plain. Is it the way they carry themselves, clothes, attitude, focus, flow with environment, or a particular behavior? Pay attention to those who don't attract attention and learn from them - study them. Be aware of everything, small and subtle behaviors can equate to large perceptions.

When you study successful gray man techniques you attain data points for future reference. Being a people watcher is helpful when integrating gray man tactics, but its uses are not limited there. In everyday life, awareness of others gives much needed information to solve problems - to become more efficient. Gray man tactics help in understanding and predicting real time events. The military calls live scenarios "real world events", this requires you to be integrated into the environment to make sound judgements. You wouldn't want to make decisions with only a partial understanding. With your awareness, position yourself to collect the most information before having to make a decision. This will become easier in time, but for now let it develop.

Why be Gray?

The short answer of why be gray is personal safety. At times you may throttle up or down the intensity, but being gray can provide a way out of harm (in certain environments and situations). Being gray is not a lifestyle but something you do to preserve it. Safeguards come in many forms, being gray is one of those. Lending to safety and security, the practice expands the effectiveness of most operational objectives.

The gray man creates advantages within the element of surprise. The concealed nature of identity, skill, and mindset provide a reserve capacity useful in overcoming challenges. The further you develop gray man tactics the further you build certainty in shaping your way in life. Certainty increases the more you are in tune with your environment and self.

Being gray provides a level of crime prevention, you avoid threats by not being viewed as a viable target. The gray man buys time through awareness and planning to counter threats. This is as simple as knowing when to leave an area, or how to gather information to deescalate a situation. Small choices acted upon at the right time can redirect or cancel out larger (negative) outcomes.

The state of grayness minimizes the probability of becoming a victim of a crime. Criminals typically seek those who are easily taken advantage of. The gray man is not flashy, self-absorbed, or arrogant. They don't walk in places that get you robbed, expose yourself helplessly, and act in a manner that encourages crimes of opportunity. They use common sense. They don't walk alone at night in high crime areas with expensive clothing and accessories. Ladies, don't wear seductive clothing, if so, expect guys to give you attention. Also expect that you are getting attention from others you may not see, those that are waiting to take advantage of you against your consent.

Be mindful of how you may be politically profiled and how this could cause harm. Know what sites are safe when on the web before you go to them. Know who you're talking to when using technology, there are many ways scammers can deceive you. Cybercrimes happen mainly from what you did or did not do.

Extortion, identity theft, and mail theft can be minimized by making personal information more secure. This goes for the more hardcore crimes as well, such as grand theft auto and home invasion. In most scenarios you have a hand in the outcome, so become aware that what you do has consequences.

Societal calamities can be made less severe when practicing gray man tactics. Economic, ecological, and political crisis's can be a source of great stress for prolonged periods. These may produce social unrest and rule without law scenarios. War times may include rationing due to a lack of resources. Natural and man-made disasters can displace thousands if not millions of people in short periods of time. What about pandemics? It is important to consider the possible and have a plan. If not you will suffer.

As you can imagine, things can always get worse. But having the ability to blend in and get lost in the masses can benefit you in the most difficult of situations. Whether it be at home, in your car, at work, or while on vacation - everyone needs to consider what is going on around them. Many times just being discreet will be the ticket to safety. But for other times when the need is greater, look to history for answers. What will happen has in some form already happen before. What we need to realize is that details make a difference.

If there is a food shortage, it doesn't make sense to tell your neighborhood that you have food if you want to eat. If you have an expensive vehicle, it does not make sense to park it on the street and not in your garage. If you have expensive collectibles, don't let those on the sidewalk see them through your windows. Most of what it is to be gray is common sense, keep issues simple and decisions will be less complicated.

The gray man uses the element of surprise, prevention, awareness, avoidance, modesty, mindfulness, and discreetness to prevail even in the worst of environments. Practice these traits as gray man tactics.

Gray Man Camouflage Tactics

"What you do speaks so loudly that I cannot hear what you say."
– Ralph Waldo Emerson

Camouflage is not just something the military or hunters use, we can benefit from it too. The topic of camouflage in this section concerns the ability to conceal what is of interest. In each section reflect on the concept of OPSEC to maximize results. There are many aspects of active and passive camouflage, let's start at home.

At home you may feel the safest but are you? Are you doing things that may compromise your safety or the safety of your family? Looking in from the outside, what do you notice about your neighborhood? Is there more activity at certain times of the day, certain days of the week? Pay attention to your immediate neighbors and how their behaviors may affect you. Are your neighbors attracting the wrong attention, doing things that make you less safe? Look at the perimeter of your property, is there a barrier between the street and your house? How easy is it to go from the street to your front door? How secure is your garbage, are you mindful of what is put into the garbage and how it could be used against you?

One low tech approach to property security is using landscaping to restrict access. A funnel effect with the use of trees, bushes, and fencing helps to route intruders to optimum defensive locations. Thorny bushes and large boulders make for ideal natural defenses to protect sensitive locations.

How much privacy does your home afford? What can you deduce by driving or walking by your home? If using binoculars what could a person see? Do you keep window treatments closed? Can a stranger see desirable things outside or inside of your home? Do you have any attention getting features on your property? Do you display a controversial sign, flag, or an element of high contrast?

Is the color scheme of the home ordinary or do people stop and look? Does your house look overly fortified with tall fences, gates, cameras, motion sensors, security doors, alarm company signs, and guard dogs? While it is smart to approach personal security in layers, make it as discreet as possible. You don't want to look like an easy target for criminals, but you also don't want to look like your trying to protect something of high value.

Active security lighting, random activities, and consistent vigilance makes for a less desirable target. Those who are looking to do a home invasion will have less interest if they have difficulty getting to the front door and being exposed via cameras or detection systems. Keep nice high dollar possessions private and secure. This includes vehicles, jewelry, electronics, and tools. Secure extra cash and jewelry in a safe and keep garage and shop doors closed as to not advertise ownership of expensive and desirable tools. Always be mindful of those looking to take what is not theirs. Many situations invite crimes of opportunity, these tempting scenarios can be eliminated with a little forethought and attention.

Outside of the home most people spend a bulk of their time at work. Work means different things to different people, some work at one location while others travel. For those who are at one location, you may be able to enhance your security and privacy because you're in a less exposed environment. This is in contrast to those who are constantly moving through public spaces. Gray man principles can be used at home and at work. Be aware of the environmental baseline, identify the flow, and recognize who is and who is not trustworthy. Even if you trust a coworker there is no need to brag about personal possessions, revealing sensitive personal information, flaunt talents or skills, or expose capabilities outside of those used for work. At work be relaxed and enjoyable to be around, be respected because you are respectful to others. Don't be meddlesome and you won't attract meddling people.

Behavior is important because it includes the way you carry yourself, how and what you say, how you groom yourself, and what you wear. These are all important in delivering subtle but refined results. You don't want to be viewed as a snob or a bum. Tattoos, excessive piercings, and even birthmarks can create contrast with others or an environment. Find ways to conceal these features when possible to minimize attention. Becoming gray requires awareness in fashion and of your mannerisms. Most people don't really know how they come off to others, so become more aware of this. Ask close friends and family members you trust for genuine feedback. Get advice in needed areas.

Avoid isolating yourself and looking or acting withdrawn. Withdrawal makes you more conspicuous, something the gray man avoids. Lone individuals are more likely to be noticed and remembered than a quiet member in a group. The better you fit in the more invisible you are to those around you. Avoid detailed conversations and use common politeness, that's enough. If you have an issue with someone and it requires a solution, talk directly to them about it. Talking negatively about someone brings more attention to you than them. Treat others as you would want to be treated. You don't want to be the center of attention, but at the same time not someone looking like they are avoiding it too. When alone in public spaces sit and stand near others. Avoid sitting in the front or back row of a room. Sit somewhere in the middle and closer to the side that is nearest to an exit. Teachers and presenters typically are more apt to call on those in the back of class, and to look more at those in the front than those elsewhere. Look busy taking notes or doing something else (do what is appropriate in your environment) to prevent others from approaching you if that is what is desired.

Behavior in combination with personal presentation is what is seen by others. Increase your awareness of your mannerisms and features by looking in a mirror, recording your voice, having someone record you as you interact with others, and start looking at what other people are doing in reaction to your behavior. It's also noteworthy to expand your viewpoints on how you are seen by strangers - what their first impressions are. You can do this by having a friend introduce you to a friend of theirs that you have never met. After an afternoon with this new person ask them how you were perceived. They may be reluctant to tell you everything out of embarrassment, but you may get new insights. Being gray is not about being unique, it's just the opposite. Many people thrive on their ego of being distinctive, this initially makes adapting gray man tactics difficult.

The most common behaviors that cause people to notice you are those outside the environmental flow. Generally speaking, if your child starts screaming they will get attention if no other child is screaming. If you are the only person to lay down on a sidewalk people will look. If you start talking to yourself or look disheveled you may get stares. Humans are social creatures keen to the baseline of what is and what is not normal. Awareness and expectations are heightened in some environments over others. A person walking into Walmart to buy milk and bread is not expected to look dressed up as someone going to a formal dinner. The gray man needs to be proficient in blending in – different places require different approaches.

Use the input you have gathered to compile a gray man version of yourself. This may require a dramatic change in hairstyle, wardrobe, and word choice. Don't make all the changes at once, only change one or two things a week. Over the course of several months you will be well on your way.

Hair is a large factor, there are so many ways men and women can configure it. You can change color, let it grow out, cut it short, or just give it a trim. Some styles look better on some people than on others, so you may have to experiment to find what works best if you haven't already. Generally speaking in most parts of the world women have longer hair then men. Avoid unnatural hair colors and styles, men should keep facial hair simple and well groomed.

Clothing is a major means of expression for many people. Outside of how you manage your body, clothing is the subsequent means to blend in with your environment. If at a sports game wear the colors of your team. If in public consider neutral earth tones if a color scheme is not already designated. Browns, greens, blues, grays, and off-whites are sure choices for most locations and situations. In most environments avoid outfits using a single color and loud attention getting plaids and stripes. Be mindful of how to blend your outfit with those around you to look obscure. Be aware of how selected garments interact with other items on your person. Don't allow your firearm or any other self-defense tool to print through your clothing. The element of surprised is your friend. Black or dark colored t-shirts help to break up printing when concealing a firearm or other gear.

Shoes and accessories can bring undesired attention - be careful not to overdue. Hats should be simple with no lettering and logos unless at a specific event with others wearing the same. Headwear can be used to counter elevated video surveillance cameras by providing a level of privacy with the use of brimmed hats. Belts should be simple in construction and ordinary in color, examples include black, brown, and earth tones. Pants should not look overly tactical, a utilitarian approach works best in most environments. In casual settings jeans without holes and dyed in common colors are preferable and are generally accepted. Shoes and socks should be plain and not advertise name brands. In many cases generic shoe brands work just as well as name brands. Dark colored shoes typically draw less attention then brighter colored ones. Watches, cell phones, and eyewear should look plain and simple. Don't wear flashy jewelry or items of any real value. Use a standard low cost smart phone that would be less desirable to a thief. Change your look with non-prescription or prescription glasses, contacts, sunglasses, reversible jackets, neckwear, and the addition or subtraction of low profile accessories. Eyewear should be dark enough to protect your eyes from the sun and to conceal where you're looking. Select non reflective polarized impact resistant lens for best results. Big mirror-like reflective sunglasses draw attention and look aggressive.

Keep your wallet in a forward body position for easier access and protection. In higher risk environments consider a decoy wallet and secondary self-defense option. Position at least one self-defense tool accessible by either hand. If pinned down on your strong side this allows you to access a weapon on your weak side.

Scent control is an important element not to be overlooked, smell is one of the senses most linked to memory. Be as scent neutral as possible. Scents help to recall past memories and create contrast in environments. The best solution is to have no memorable smell. Be aware of your body odor, deodorants, fabric softeners, cologne, body sprays, perfumes, soaps, lotions, and food that may be associated with you.

It's a good habit to stay streamlined in what and how you carry on your person. It's also smart to carry items that have multiple uses. An example would include carrying a multitool to replace a knife, pliers, screwdriver, and wire cutters. Sometimes all you need is the right tool and not four or five separate implements.

Don't carry excessive or conspicuous gear when traveling. Keep tourist related items concealed and follow local customs, costume, and mannerisms. Be aware of local gestures that are considered disrespectful and insulting. In most environments a conservative look is best. Less is more and relaxed is better than looking tense. Learn basic greetings and generic sayings when traveling in new locations you're not accustomed to. Causal conversational skills are beneficial not only in helping to interact with locals for directions and ordering food, but to summons help. In some cultures body language and speaking volume are large factors in communication. It's not always what you say that matters but how you say it. Don't look lost even if you are, you will become more vulnerable by those looking for an easy target.

What about active camouflage? Active camouflage is a type of adaptable concealment which helps to safeguard high value targets. A form of active camouflage includes blending resources under the cover of ordinary use. Let's say you want to store 10,000 gallons of water in water tanks behind your house. If you did this it would look suspicious and people would start talking. How else could you store water? Answer: swimming pool or pond. If that's not realistic make it seem you need water tanks for your gardens. Just make sure you have gardens large enough to justify the storage. You could also use low profile rain barrels, underground cisterns, or water containers stored in your garage. When needed, use active camouflage to justify actions and conceal resources – sometimes in plain view.

When hiding items of significance consider decoy locations and ordinary items or spaces. Small objects could be stashed in a planter, the dead space of furniture or cabinets, bottom of waste baskets, and in walls or vents. Use diversion to mask high contrasting items as plain and uninteresting. Tone down the level of stimulus to minimize level of attention. An example could be storing something of value in an old cardboard box as you transport it to another location. Old luggage, a pile of clothes, or a weathered shoe box are other options usable for concealment.

It's wise and advised not to live beyond your means. Living on credit cards and other debt only bring hardship and negative outcomes. Be debt free whenever possible and learn how to restrain buying impulses. Never stop learning, understand that knowledge is power. Look at the big picture before investing large amounts of time, energy, and money. Save and invest early in life and have adequate insurance coverage. The number one cause of bankruptcy is unexpected healthcare cost. Be responsible with any extra money you receive or earn. Hold on to your house and vehicles if they meet your needs. Moving and buying new vehicles every few years is expensive and excessive – certainly not necessary.

The gray man is a private person – they keep personal matters private. The gray man practices self-defense techniques quietly and out of the view of the public. If using a public facility the gray man goes at the least busy times. The gray man does not linger at stores, they acquire what is needed and move on. The gray man allows others to overestimate themselves, to become overly confident – they use inflated ego and the element of surprise as a means of protection. The gray man does not telegraph movement nor intent. They are invisible unless desired to be known. The gray man never draws attention by word, dress, action, or mannerism. The gray man should be underestimated in abilities. Don't look weak or too strong - you will attract the attention of others. It's better not to leave an impression - keep eye contact at a minimum, eye contact stimulates the brain which forms memories. When encountering a person for the first time, don't trap them in a space - give them room and a way out. Avoid the police when possible, many are confrontational which brings unwanted attention.

When should you use a self-defense weapon? This is an important question. The gray man never exposes a weapon unless it lessens the chance of being a target or victim. Only use concealed weapons when a threat is eminent to wellbeing. It's smart to carry both non-lethal and lethal weapons to maximize your self-defense options. In a court of law using a non-lethal option before a lethal option shows restraint. The more you can show that you had no other recourse, and you were in real danger - the better your case will look. Be open to the use of off label items for self-defense; such as baseball bats, scissors, flashlights, hammers, screwdrivers, and briefcase. With that being said, your primary defense should always be awareness. The more aware the harder it is to become a victim. All it takes is a gun to your head for someone to take all you own. This could be avoided with situational awareness. Practice and planning can get you through the bulk of issues if combined with awareness.

How should you practice situational awareness? A good start is keeping track of what is occurring in your proximity. Keep from getting distracted with music, electronics, and repetitive thinking. Be mindful not to daydream or get sluggish. Stay as alert as possible without looking out of place. Sit up tall and avoid slouching. Don't nap in public, it may feel safe but your exposed more than you may realize.

Always assume someone is watching. Don't get sucked into your phone or have long conversations on it in public. Keep your head up and moving. Eyes able to see are more useful than those looking down to the ground. Listen to the sounds as you move through spaces. What are people talking about? Can you make out what they are saying? Is there anything that stands out? Look when someone enters a room, this is always a smart behavior. If you notice a threat just as it enters a room, you have more time to react than those oblivious. Don't forget to use your sense of smell to retrieve memories. When indoors, keep tabs on what's going on outside via windows and opened doorways. Practice these techniques until they become natural to you.

Observation and information collection are gray man specialties. Learn to observe your surroundings discreetly. Leverage peripheral vision and use decoy objects to give an impression that attention is directed on a neutral object. Reading a newspaper, magazine, word puzzle or using a cell phone make great decoy objects. These ordinary activities allows surveying of an area and thus collection of information. Eyewear that hides your eyes will allow you the freedom to scan rapidly without attracting attention. Use the stimuli in your environment to act in less noticeable ways. Cover your movements via noise from traffic, local construction activity, or the playing of music in public venues. Using local ambient noise is helpful when needing to mask noises. HVAC condensers and other common noise sources such as sirens can drown out glass breaking and doors being kicked in.

Don't stare and linger - look at targets passively and flowingly. People take notice of what others notice, be mindful of where you point your face and eyes. By you looking at something outside the baseline, others will look and bring attention to you. It's best to not look like you're taking notice of anything in particular. Indirectly look at targets through materials, natural movements, and scanning techniques. An example includes looking at a store display and paying attention to the reflections in the glass. This provides needed information of your surroundings (what's behind you) through indirect means. Another means involves your shoes. Tying your shoe allows you to stop, bend over, and turn slightly to one side – all possibly desirable actions when gathering information. Movements may need to drop below eye level to avoid detection, or to buy time for further information gathering. Holding a door for a group allows you time to scan a space in a natural manner. As you open and close the door you have an opportunity to see a wide angle view of your location.

Crossing a street should be thought through before doing. If evading others be mindful of how crossing a street could expose you. One method to minimize presence is to cross a roadway out of sight of others. This may be in a bend or dip in the road. Look and listen in both directions for signs of incoming vehicles. Stay low to the ground and move fast to the other side of the road. Use shadows or low light areas to further minimize visual contrast. By using a bend or depression in the road you help to obscure the crossing and thus avoid detection. Make sure to find sections of the road that contain cover on both sides, this aids in concealing yourself before and after crossing.

Don't be a fly on the wall, be the wall. First impressions last and matter, so don't make an impression. Don't stand out, be forgettable. This conflicts with modern day thinking that we all should be outwardly unique. The gray man is not interested in what others think, they are not trendsetters - they have control over their ego.

Once again, avoid eye contact when possible. You're more memorable when you give direct eye contact to those you are communicating with. What you do and how you do it is the easiest way to tip off a trained observer. Through the use of observing demeanor one can spot baseline deviations contrasting with the flow of the surroundings. This is why it's important to do what others are as you navigate through a location. When moving about be aware of the established baseline and determine an operational risk assessment. Questions should include: Does the risk outweigh the cost? Are you taking unnecessary risks? Do you have a plan to anticipate and manage the risk? Does your plan involve an in depth, deliberate, and time critical formula? Ask yourself questions such as these in unfamiliar locations, these help identify best actions coinciding with present order and rhythm. Look uninterested, calm, and moderately comfortable when in public. The more unassuming you look the better.

Gray Man Safety

"For safety is not a gadget but a state of mind." – Eleanor Everet

First and foremost safety has much to do if not entirely about awareness. Situational awareness is when one is cognizant of what is going on around them. This state creates opportunities when actively interacting with your environment. The more aware, the more time you gain to react to happenings around you. Without awareness things happen without warning. Being caught off guard is not a trait of the gray man.

It's been said that safety is as simple as ABC – Always Be Careful. But is it really that easy to be careful? Life can get busy and thus be full of distraction, so how do you deal with this and still be safe? One simple approach is to slow down and reduce the activities you are engaged with. Another bit of advice is don't be at the right place at the wrong time. This is sometimes obvious while other times unavoidable. Take for example going out late at night to get snacks at your local gas station. If this said gas station has a history of late night crime it would be best to avoid such place. But what about situations we find ourself in that are unavoidable? For these occasions we need to pull from skills and available resources for solutions. Problem solving skills will need to be utilized, this is best done while remaining calm.

Let's take a look at common everyday resources useful in self-defense. The most common items at our disposal are those thing that we wear, carry, or keep close at hand. Examples of these items include:

Ball Cap – create a distraction by throwing a ball cap in an aggressors face, this may buy time to make the most of a defensive or offensive tactic

Belt – leather belts make for a strong and durable means to keep others at distance or to strike with when faced with one or more attackers

Bobby Pins – the longer and thicker the pins the better for grasping and striking an attacker in the ears and eyes

Chopstick Style Hair Pins – strong bamboo, wood, or metal chopstick hair pins are useful for striking and pressure point compliance

Eyewear – protect the eyes from impact threats with impact rated eyewear (ANSI Z87.1 or Z87+ ratings) as well as concealing the eyes to minimize telegraphing intention

Jacket – protecting hands and arms when threatened with sharp objects is made possible via wrapping body parts with a jacket

Keychain Bottle Top Opener – bottle cap openers with pointed tips make for an effective striking and scraping self-defense tool

Keyring or Keychain – using your keys and a lanyard fob can quickly be put into action when swung in the face of an attacker as a strike or a means to create distance

Metal Nail File – useful as a blunt striking tool, the nail file can be used to defend with strikes to soft body tissue

Scissors – while we may not carry scissors on our person a pair is typically nearby in the home or office, use this tool to stab and or deter a threat

Shoes – pointed shoes or steel toed footwear gives options when striking an aggressor via kicks

Another strategy within self-defense is the use of misdirection. The human brain is wired to fill the gaps between seeing and believing. Use the gap from what people see and what they think they see. Shape the narrative around the misdirection. Shaping involves words, placement of people and things, subtle actions and suggestions, and your story or doing to lead the person(s) to fill in the gap that you created. Control the focus of your opponent, allow them to act on your behalf unknowingly. Small actions such as a gentle touch, glance, reshifting of the body, or release of breath at the right time can be the difference of controlling focus or not. Misdirection could allow you to escape a dangerous situation or help others facing a threat. Direct your opponents through the illusion of agency (free will). The best traps are set with techniques where the opponent walks into willingly. Half-truths and partial cooperation can slow an aggressor to buy time for an opportunity to make a beneficial move. The more the opponent believes it's their choice to do something the more energy they will commit to what you want them to do. Employ the familiar, take secret advantage of habits, patterns, and expectations. Build on each misdirection for maximum results. Several subtle misdirection's can form a large effect. Always have a backup plan and an out. Being several steps ahead of your opponent gives you room to adapt to a changing situation.

The following are examples of items useful when misdirecting, they include common items used in subtle ways. One of my favorites is the decoy wallet, this can deescalate a situation quickly and leave you with no real loss. There are many approaches on how to set up a decoy wallet, just remember to not include any identifying information or anything of real value. A common way people configure their decoy wallet is with a few dollars, a few random business cards, and a credit card. The credit card will have its origins from an active card in your real wallet. Report this card stolen and request a replacement. Be sure to sand off your name, signature, and some of your account numbers before storing in your decoy wallet. This technique allows the criminal to be tracked if attempted to be used. If you are not comfortable with this approach then just leave out the credit card. Another aspect to consider is the wallet, what type would best serve you. In my opinion a lightweight nylon wallet with a closure zipper is comfortable to carry and effective. It's effective because of two subtle traits, containment and simplicity. Having a zippered wallet keeps everything in during carry and may buy you time if the perpetrator opens to look in. In many cases the perpetrator when faced with a zipper will not be able to effectively open the wallet because one hand may be holding a weapon. In this case the criminal may simply leave because they think they got what they wanted. A zippered wallet can easily be transferred to another pocket or pack without worry of items being lost. One tactic used when in a confrontation is throwing the decoy wallet away from you and running in the opposite direction. If this is something you plan on doing consider a brighter color decoy wallet. By having something easily seen in low light conditions, the perpetrator will have an easier time seeing and finding it when thrown.

Additional items useful for misdirection include the cane, walking stick, umbrella, rolled up newspaper, metal ink pen, clothing, money, and food. As you can imagine, some of these items are useful for self-defense as others are ways to distract. Some direct means of getting attention may involve the use of animals, voice, environmentally contrasting behavior, personal alarms, vehicle horn, and the use of a whistle. The use of these examples can aid in your misdirection efforts for an end goal of personal safety.

Let's now look at a list of common self-defense gear. Many of these purpose built items require training to effectively use, so keep that in mind after purchasing.

Baton

Blades folding and fixed

Club

Firearm

Kubaton

Pepper / OC spray, foam or gel

Self-defense keychain tools

Stun gun

Tactical crenulated flashlight

Taser

For those looking for more exotic options, examples of less common self-defense tools include:

Concealed bladed comb

Defensive umbrella / walking stick (this product is reinforced and built to strike with)

Monkey fist on a lanyard

Polymer edged weapon / pressure point pain compliance tool

Spike pen (penetrator tool with hollow shaft to disable vehicles (tires and radiator))

Stun gun cane

Stun gun knuckles

Stun gun staff

Tactical pen

Weighted ball caps

Weighted slap sticks

Additional gear useful in an off label use for self-defense include:

Golf ball in a pair of stockings

Hammer

Ice pick

Kitchen gear and utensils

Large nails

Parachute cord

Screwdriver

Shemagh

Finally, what are your options when material resources are limited or not available? During desperate times your body can be used as a weapon. Hand to hand combative skills are essential when manipulating aggressors. This is especially true when you are fighting for your life. We all have a right to self-preservation, thus it's vital to learn combative techniques. The following are basic combative techniques that are easy to remember and carry out:

Striking the attacker with cupped hands over both ears simultaneously. This will cause disorientation, ringing in the ears, nausea, and possibly bleeding and intense pain in the inner ear.

Striking the attacker on the Adam's apple (laryngeal prominence). This may cause choking and thus make the attacker pull back or retreat.

Striking the attacker square in the nose with an open palm. This may cause severe damage and pain to the nose area depending on force applied. An open palm strike delivers more energy and pressure than a closed fist.

Striking the attacker in the soft tissue void under the Adam's apple. This will cause a gag or choking reflex, this may buy you time to make another more devastating strike or to escape the threat.

Striking the attacker in the knee from the front or side. This will cause pain and possible knee injury limiting mobility. Kicking the knee may result in permanent damage.

Striking the attacker in the shin. This will cause pain and distract the individual while you make other strikes or leave the area.

Striking the attacker in the eyes with one or two fingers. This will disorient their visual field and possibly cause temporary or even permanent blindness. The use of objects such as a writing utensil can be used to reach the eyes.

Grabbing and twisting the attacker's nose and ears. This can be used to create pain compliance or temporary discomfort. This technique is useful during a scuffle.

Winning People Over

"Be civil to all; sociable to many; familiar with few; friend to one; enemy to none." – Benjamin Franklin

There are many practices when dealing with others which yield useful outcomes. This section will review techniques that help to win others over.

Winning people over starts with connection. A simple ice breaker is used to search for shared experiences. People relax and identify with those more like themselves. Winning people over is not a form of manipulation, but of building relationships to give reason to warrant respect. You want others to respect you so that they want to engage with you. Respect is earned from consistency in action and charity to others. Listening skills are a major factor in gathering information and engaging with others when building rapport. You have to be engaging to win others over, being passive is not effective. Patience is another positive behavior which is rewarded with friendship and trust. Patience can be demonstrated through positive collaborations with those you're winning over. Having agreeable values and positive intentions also helps to build a more genuine rapport. A compassionate person who principals are chiefly concerned about the dignity of others will be noticed and supported. It's what you know and what you do with it for others that matters. A great way to make good impressions is by getting your hands dirty – do the work with others. Share in the challenges and develop a history of success with those you are wanting to win over. A shared positive history is a strong foundation to build on.

As you win people over it's helpful to know how to handle them. To start, avoid saying and doing things which make people defensive. This typically comes from criticism, condemnation, and complaining. Build others up rather than tear them down. Honest and sincere appreciation invites meaningful sharing and personal growth. Find common ground to merge your wants with their wants. A unified front is more powerful and influential in getting results. Avoid arguments, show respect and never say to another that they are wrong. People very much dislike hearing they are wrong. Instead, provide evidence that there is another answer. If you identify that you're in the wrong admit to this quickly and emphatically. An easy going friendly demeanor is what most people prefer. You can prime people to like you by using unconscious suggestions. For example, start a conversation with questions that you know will end in yes. Having a person say yes out loud several times relaxes and reinforces that you are safe and agreeable. Let others do the bulk of the talking. If you bring up an idea that resonates with another person, let them feel that it's their idea. Look at the world from the other person's perspective. Be sympathetic to others ideas and desires, people crave sympathy from others. Appeal to nobler motives. People like to believe that they are noble and morally upright. Don't limit how you communicate with others. Dramatize your ideas by being vivid and expressive. Allow others to be expressive too – personal growth results from healthy challenges. The more you facilitate growth in others the deeper your connection.

What about ways to increase your likability?

People will like you if you become genuinely interested in them. Asking about them and spending time with them are sure ways to build likeability.

Smile – it's a simple but revealing gesture that signals goodwill.

Say their name - people love to hear their name. Say it often when you spend time with them. People also enjoy hearing that you like them, you trust them, they look good, they are funny, you are thankful, and words of encouragement. People likewise appreciate positive references and actions that build esteem.

Listen – encourage others to talk about themselves. Listen more than you speak. Understand what they are saying. Many of the times people don't want conversation but to be listened to.

Talk about topics of mutual interest. What are the shared passions?

Make people feel important – be sincere. Treat others as you would want to be treated.

How do you change (or influence) others and still be liked if in a leadership position?

Begin with praise and honest appreciation.

Call attention to mistakes or weaknesses indirectly.

Talk about your own mistakes before highlighting theirs.

Ask questions and educate over giving orders.

Let the person save face. Always discipline others in private.

Use encouragement – make faults seem easy to correct.

Praise improvements – reward progress when possible.

Give the person a respectable reputation. People tend to do what they believe is expected from them.

Be flexible – people respect those who are less rigid but assertive. If you're too aggressive people get defensive.

Use intuition to build trust through concession rather than argumentation.

Deception Detection

"The truth is a lot easier to see when you stop assuming you already have it." – Mike Norton

Deducing whether someone is lying is tricky and not always straightforward. The following information can help in spotting a liar.

Create a baseline – ask a few questions with predictable results. Compare behavior and mannerisms to later questions to identify lies. If behaviors are noticeably different they may be uncomfortable to the question or simply lying. Ask questions in three different ways, this will approach the question at different angles to subtly bypass a guarded liar.

A behavior pause or delay – if too much thought has to be made to answer a question it might be a lie.

Verbal / non-verbal disconnect – this includes hiding eyes and mouth as well as nodding yes when saying no and vice versa. Mismatched behaviors point to a possible truth discrepancy.

Throat clearing and heavy swallowing – done before answering a question is a possible indication that a person is going to lie. This is sometimes done to buy time to create a lie or an expression of anxiety.

Hand to face activity – biting nails and lips, licking the lips, pulling the lips and ears, and rubbing the eyes and nose. Engorged blood in the nose causing a nose itch is common when people lie.

Wringing or rubbing of the hands – this may indicate fidgeting or anxiety from deceitfulness.

Self-grooming to manage sweat or to conceal anxiety is a red flag that someone is possibly lying. Behaviors such as manipulating items in the room without reason is also suspicious.

Inappropriate emotion – laughing or smiling when they should be upset. Blatant inconsistencies, suspicious expressions, unnecessary superlatives, blushing, excessive blinking, flared nostrils, and fake smiles are all possible indications of dishonestly. If the emotions don't match the situation the person could be acting deceitfully.

Shutting down or wanting to move on to a different topic may indicate the hiding of truth or the start of being insincere.

Phrases such as "In all candor", "If I'm being completely truthful", and "If I had to swear on a stack of bibles" point to the activity of deceitfulness. If you have to emphasize you're telling the truth you might not be telling the truth. Also be on the lookout for excessive use of the word "no".

Inconsistencies in stories and not being able to remember or repeat previously told details and concepts are red flag indicators. If a person can one day clearly remember specific details but not the next, this may point to deceitfulness.

Here are some famous quotes concerning deception:

"Be not deceived with the first appearance of things, for show is not substance." – English Proverb

"The greatest deception men suffer is from their own opinions."
– Leonardo da Vinci

"All deception in the course of life is indeed nothing else but a lie reduced to practice, and falsehood passing from words into things."
– Robert Southey

"Cunning is the art of concealing our own defects, and discovering the weaknesses of others." – William Hazlitt

"It seems to me that there are two kinds of trickery: the "fronts" people assume before one another's eyes, and the "front" a writer puts on the face of reality." – Francoise Sagan

"Nothing is more common on earth than to deceive and be deceived."
– Johann G. Seume

"The easiest way to be cheated is to believe yourself to be more cunning than others." – Pierre Charron

"Tricks and treachery are the practice of fools, that don't have brains enough to be honest." – Benjamin Franklin

"We are never deceived; we deceive ourselves." – Johann Wolfgang von Goethe

"You can fool some of the people all the time, and all of the people some of the time, but you cannot fool all of the people all the time." – Abraham Lincoln

Gray Man Everyday Carry

Everyone has different needs to efficiently navigate through their day, thus the items we carry on our person will vary. Outside of specialized carry gear, most people carry a similar core of essentials. Here are common carry items useful for the gray man:

Bandanas / handkerchiefs are handy items to have in a variety of situations. Used to wipe the face of sweat or manage a leaky nose - any color of cotton bandana will do. For signaling and attention getting a brightly colored bandana is ideal. Bandanas can also be used as tinder, water prefilters, and bandages.

Battery banks are available in compact offerings - ideal for everyday carry. When a primary power source is exhausted, switch over to your backup. A battery bank can provide axillary power to critical devices. This extends your capability and provides a resource to make emergency calls, or to power up other needed devices over extended periods of time. There are adaptors available that allow various types of batteries such as a common CR123 battery to be plugged into your phone. This makes for a small but powerful backup energy resource.

Candy, gum, and food bars are handy to have when delayed in traffic and when access to food is limited or not available. There are many benefits from having extra calories and nutrients during an emergency. For example, diabetics sometimes have sugar crashes and may need a helping hand. Carrying a few pieces of hard candy may be all that is needed to save the day.

Clothing is important to a gray man mainly because it helps them to blend in and be adaptive. Convertible, reversible, and concealment type clothing are good options to have on hand. A reversible hat, shirt, and jacket are great ways to change your look quickly without having to carry additional clothing. Pants that convert into shorts change your profile without much effort. Eyewear with replaceable lens are ideal when needing to change the look or profile of the face.

Cutting tools are essential for many people while at home or when at work. Uses range from simple cutting of boxes and rope to lifesaving extraction. One of the first things to decide on is the format of carry - a folder or fixed blade? The most common option is the pocket knife, this is because they tend to be concealable and lightweight. A compact fixed blade such as a neck knife, is another popular choice for those looking for minimum weight and bulk. Depending on your price range the type and quality of knife will vary dramatically. Three things to first look at in a knife is blade steel, blade grind, and aesthetics in hand. Much of the cutting capability comes from the blade material and blade geometry. You may also pay attention to the overall attention to detail, handle materials, and the means to secure it to your person. There are many things to consider, allocate time to research the best product to fit your needs. Remember that your blade choice will be a daily companion, an investment which will yield many years of use if cared for. After decades of experimenting, here are my preferences for a folding blade: under 3 ounces, handle length of 4 to 4.5 inches, uses a blade steel that is resistant to rust and holds and edge (154CM / VG-10 / CPM S30V / H1 / 14C28N, and 420HC). I prefer blades which use a flat or saber grind, and incorporates handle scales made from G10 or FRN (fiberglass reinforced nylon). Trial and error over time will yield a criteria for your ideal blade, so keep up the search.

Firestarters may not sound needed if you're a non-smoker, but the uses are numerous. While you may not use a lighter daily you may be glad you have one if certain situations occurred. For most, the lighter is a preferred means of making fire due to ease of use and small form factor. But if you prefer a different type of firestarter then carry that. The ability to make fire gives you light, heat, and a means to signal. When needed, controlled fire making can be also a means of creating a distraction. The gray man is a catalyst of possibilities, thus the fundamental ability to make fire on demand is essential.

First aid supplies carried on the person aids in comfort and survivability during a medical emergency. A simple loadout includes a few compact bandages, compact tourniquet, and several medical gloves. Realistically most people don't carry these items, but it's possible to do if committed. The majority of the time you will have no use for your medical supplies. But in those rare moments when life is threatened, you will find peace in having what was needed.

Keychains filled with keys grant us access into a medley of locations, but for many there is more. Keychain accessories are abundant providing numerous practical applications. The gray man seeks the practical so look at small, lightweight options to enhance your capability. Micro lights, mini tools, and memory sticks are just some items to consider.

Less than lethal self-defense tools are highly recommended and are a practical means to deescalate situations. Gear to consider include pepper spray /gel, OC spray, kubaton, taser, tactical pen, collapsible baton, and a tactical flashlight with crenulated bezel. Training with these items are critical, so get experience with these items before carrying them.

Lethal protection options are typically inclusive of handguns and blades. In most situations it's best to conceal all weapons as it reduces attention and secures the element of surprise. Stealth matters in personal protection. What handgun should you carry? Handguns ultimately come in two flavors, revolvers and semi-automatics. Depending on preference and needs the type of handgun can be determined. Those in low risk environments may want the simplicity of a revolver, while others may want more capacity and the form factor found in semi-automatics. Most people prefer semi-automatics because they are faster to reload and once again – they typically hold more ammunition. Concerning self-defense blades, these are a viable option for close encounters in which firearms may not be deployable. It's commonly underestimated the devastation of a blade in the hands of a well-trained person. In some cases a blade is more effective at stopping a threat than a bullet. It's important to keep as much distance from you and your attacker(s) as possible. When forced into close quarter conflicts a blade and hand to hand combatives are typically your last line of defense.

Light sources are not only practical for finding the keyhole on your front door; but useful in identify threats, creating distractions, and signaling. For the gray man, the ability to influence their environment is fundamental. Lights capable of producing both white and red light are recommended. Red filters can be purchased for many lights to make them more versatile during low light operations. Too often modern illumination tools put out too much or not the right type of light. A low output red or blue light aids in keeping a low profile. If colored light is not available use a moonlight mode or another low light setting. The gray man avoids attention by using light wisely. An easy way to layer lights on the body is to keep one in your pocket, one on your keychain, one on a breakaway necklace, and one in your backpack. The neck option would preferably have red or blue light output. Manufacturing companies with solid reputations for quality and reliability include Olight, Wowtac, Thrunite, Photon Lights, Streamlight, and Maglite. Always do your own research to verify you are getting the best gear to meet your needs.

Mobile smart phones are an immense resource and a staple for many. They allow us to communicate, navigate, record data, and to do thousands of other tasks. This important piece of kit is more of a necessity than an option in today's technological landscape. A shock and water resistant phone case is recommended to protect your phone.

Multitools are like pocket knives, numerous in their variations. Size and weight are big factors when selecting this carry item. You won't carry it if it's too bulky and too heavy. Pay attention to the quality of materials and fit and finish. Multitools should be precise, many tasks require this. Quality varies between certain brands, in some cases drastically. First you want to identify the tool implements needed to fulfill your everyday tasks. Then depending on budget select a tool after researching your options. Leatherman, Gerber, SOG, and Victorinox are the premier go to brands for quality and reliability.

Notepads are useful for non-verbal silent communication as well as fire tinder, note and map making, and stored reference material. You can wrap the notepad cover with your tape of choice, imbed fishing hooks and sewing needles, tuck in a few bandages and emergency cash, and include an emergency contact sheet. This makes for a mini multipurpose resource which can be held together with a ranger band.

Pens are handy when recording information and leaving messages. Many lightweight and compact options are available to allow for comfortable carry. Obviously not all pens are created equal, find one that will hold up to your everyday use. Fisher is one of several brands which produce quality pens with advanced ink cartridge technology. If on a budget look to the well-known Bic Round Stick, I use this option regularly and they work well. I shorten my Bic Round Stick pens by reducing the length of the ink cartridge and barrel (pen body). After shortening the pen, extract the plug from the cutoff section and place into the shortened barrel for a finished look.

Pocket and belt pouch organizers are helpful in keeping gear accessible for quick deployment. There are many companies that cater to personal organization but only a few use the highest quality materials. A popular innovative brand with many offerings is Maxpedition. This company has several lines of emphasis ranging from the tactical to the covert. Things to look for in a pouch or pocket organizing system include quality zippers, fabrics, threads, and elastic. Look at the layout, determine if the organizing approach fits your needs. Some pocket organizers are too large to fit some pockets, so always measure to know what will fit. The gray man is commonly drawn to organizers because they are useful in constructing sub kits. These compact kits range in objectives and are simple means to expand capabilities in the field.

Storage drives come in micro form factors so there are no reasons to not have one. Use your drive to store and access data in or outside the home. The gray man keeps file information encrypted as well as hidden from prying eyes. Consider storing local maps and other vital reference material on your drive in case it's needed during an emergency.

Wallets come in many forms, but go too small or too large they become less usable. Wallets can harbor an assorted array of options if strategic in approach. Consider credit card size multitools and lock pick sets, handcuff key, spare house key*, first aid items, safety pins, phone list, and other common items such as identification, bank, and business cards. In some locations it may not be legal to carry lock picks, so be aware of your local laws. One simple way to enhance privacy is to use cash and not bank cards. Some people have completely transitioned back to cash after seeing how banking institutions use and sell their transaction data. For those concerned with RFID chip bank card technology, using cash and gift cards may provide some relief. For identification cards with RFID chips a shielded wallet may be desirable. Cash should be carried not just for privacy but for times credit and debit card machines go offline. For those living close to the border with another country, it's smart to carry or have access to that countries currency. During an emergency egress you will have the means to buy essentials in the neighboring country.

*A spare house key in the wallet may not be appropriate for everyone. If the wallet ever got lost your identification would identify where you live, and thus give use to the spare house key to a potential criminal. A *better solution is to hide a key box on your property containing your house key. Store the key to the hidden key box in your wallet.*

If possible, avoid carrying around an external bag because it creates an elevated level of attention in some environments. Obviously if everyone around you is carrying a bag, then there is nothing to worry about. Just be mindful of what you carry and how it stimulates attention.

When an external bag is needed to carry additional gear; backpacks, slings, and duffle bags are commonly used due to form factor, carry comfort, accessibility, and available options. The backpack is the most popular because it provides the best overall solution to most people. The backpack has the ability to distribute weight equally on both shoulders, thus reducing stress on specific body parts. This lends inherently to a more stable platform when carrying larger and heavier loads. Backpacks designed for heftier loads include a waist belt to help transfer weight to the hips. This helps to take pressure off the shoulders and back. Many types of packs will work, a mainstream commercially available option is the most ideal. The more common the bag the more ordinary it looks. JanSport is a brand that is commonly found at many big box stores and online retailers. Look at what others are using at your location and buy something like theirs. School, work, and leisure are just a few of the themes that people use bags for. There is another option - concealment packs. Covert packs look like many of the off the shelf bags found at most sporting goods stores, but they are internally enhanced. 5.11 Tactical is a brand that makes concealment packs which contain modified and hidden compartments for customization. In essence these packs are plain on the outside but tactically organized on the inside. These low profile options have muted color schemes and typically allow for concealing a firearm and advanced methods of organizing tactical gear. Hook and loop or MOLLE fields are used to attach and organize pouches and other gear in the inner compartments. This reduces shifting and maximizes access in time critical scenarios. While more expensive, covert packs do yield advantages over traditional tactical packs. You get much of the functionality of a tactical pack but without the look.

2 way radios can be a large asset when traveling within a group. Group communicates are vital in staying organized via sharing of information. Each member when moving independently from the group should have

a radio to communicate with others. Digitally encoded transmissions help to mask those with scanners that may be listening. The use of ear and lapel speaker/microphone accessories help to keep communications more discrete.

Bandanas and shemaghs are versatile articles that are relatively small in form and low in weight. Select a color and pattern to blend in or contrast with your environment depending on intentions. It is wise to learn several uses with these articles of cloth. The uses range from urban everyday carry to wilderness survival.

Chalk is a simple and easy to carry item that can be used to mark a location, covertly communicate via code with others, and mimic markings from other sources to create distractions or confusion. Markers and tape can also be used, but chalk is typically preferred because of ease of removal. During rain or inclement weather chalk may not be ideal, use a preferred tape instead.

Clothing is helpful in not only regulating body temperature but to quickly change your look. Concealment, convertible, and reversible clothing types are recommend to keep in your pack. It may only be one or two articles, but it doesn't take much to alter your profile.

Compact radios are useful in gathering information during a crisis. Small emergency type radios with a hand crank and or solar panel are preferred to those without. Select a radio with good reception and build quality. AM, FM, and weather band transmissions are commonly used in gathering local news and alerts. More advanced radios may include shortwave, air, and public safety bands.

Cordage is multipurpose and highly recommended, select a type that will meet your needs and not be too bulky or heavy. 550 type III parachute cord is one of the better all-purpose cordage on the market. It is compact, lightweight, and strong. Always buy American made parachute cord made of nylon to ensure integrity of use. Bank line is another cordage to consider, bank line is tarred nylon twine that comes in a variety of thickness. #36 bank line is a commonly used type that yields approximately 470 linear feet per 1 pound spool, it's rated at 340 pound breaking strength. Just like parachute cord, not all bank line is created equal. Look for bank line that is deep coated and dried before being put on the spool.

Duct tape or your preferred tape for repairs and construction is a gray man essential. Gorilla tape makes a 1" compact travel size roll, this is recommended over the standard size for ease of carry. If this is still too much tape reduce it to a desirable amount. You can wrap the desired amount on an old credit card to make a custom sized spool. Tape can be used to build shelters, mark locations, leave covert messages, close or wrap a wound, and bind wrist and ankles of those that are a threat to self or others. Most tapes can even be used as tinder for an emergency fire.

Ear protection is practical gear when exposed to loud environments. They can help you get sleep or avoid earing damage when a firearm is discharged. Foam or gel inside the ear protection are recommended because they are effective and easy to store. Being able to preserve your hearing allows you to gather more information in sensory rich environments.

Electronics such as a smart phone, tablet, laptop, and other devices may be helpful in a variety of scenarios. These devices may be helpful in providing access to information or to communicate with others. This allows the possibility to make better decisions based on current and relevant information.

Eyewear is beneficial to the gray man because it not only helps to protect the eyes from blunt impact but conceals facial characteristics. Even if you already carry a pair on your person an extra pair in your pack is worthwhile. Many sunglasses are rated for impact, these would be ideal provided they are non-reflective and muted in design and color.

Firestarters and tinder is a smart addition to any carry bag. Reliable firestarters and homemade tinder is inexpensive and virtually unnoticeable in size and weight in your pack. It's piece of mind to have a backup firestarter and different types of tinder in a fire kit.

First aid and trauma kit gear is ideal to have in case of a serious incident. Trauma to the body may require immediate care to save the person's life. Basic supplies include tourniquets, trauma bandages, hemostatic agents, wound dressings, bandage wraps, and medical gloves. Expand on this foundation as you grow in medical knowledge and experience.

Food carried in a pack will most likely need to be ready to eat items. This is for practical reasons for consumption on the go. Select healthy high calorie nutrient dense foods that are enjoyable to eat. Select those with a respectable shelf life and reasonable resistant to temperature variations. There may be times when access to a meal is limited, thus having a means to maintain blood sugar levels will enhance your alertness and reactivity. Additional food carried in your pack could also be used to help others in need after a high stress event. During a survival situation food can be used as bait for trapping and fishing.

Gloves are a useful item that takes up little space and weighs only a few ounces. Select gloves with the maximum versatility. Use common sense, during the colder seasons insulated utility gloves would be more useful than hot weather utility gloves. These keep your hands warm but also practical for abrasion protection.

Headlamps are highly recommended as a primary hands free light source. The light you carry on your person should be able to handle the majority of your needs, but having a powerful multimode headlamp in the pack greatly enhances capability. A USB rechargeable headlamp is more user friendly for most, but beware, some models contain built in batteries which are not user serviceable or replaceable. An ideal setup would include a light with moonlight mode, a signal mode, several brightness settings, and the ability to remove the battery to replace if needed. Some headlamps have built in colored lens filters for specific uses in the field. The human eye is efficiently tuned to certain light wavelengths in certain conditions. Many military maps are made to be used with red and blue wavelength light. Red light is used for nighttime movement to avoid detection and to preserve night vision. Blue light is used by Special Forces because in low output it's hard to detect at distances, it's also more difficult to be detected by night vision. In addition, blue light is used by hunters and medics to identify blood trails and wound sites. Yellow or amber light is more effective than white light when moving through heavy fog. Defused low output white light is useful for up close use, filtered lens helps to modify light concentration to minimize hot spots. Defused light also helps to reduce glare and reinforce light discipline tactics. Green light works best with most night vision and adequately with many maps. Green light is one of the more visible light wavelengths and thus the reason why they are found in the brightest chemlights, lasers, and flares. Fluorescent yellow-green at about 550 nanometers is the brightest and most sensitive color to the human eye in daylight. At night orange-red is the most prominent color.

Lightweight tarps could be a vital piece of kit if you live in a rural area and have the possibility of being stranded. It's also beneficial to have a means of cover when helping someone with a traumatic injury. A tarp for example could be used to provide rain protection over a victim of a car accident. Tarps can be used as a visual barrier and as a means to collect water and carry injured people.

Maps and compasses are a smart addition to any everyday carry bag. Most people simply rely on their smart devices, but what happens when they fail or the network is down? A backup means of navigating makes sense when technology is the only factor guiding you to where you need to be. Cell service goes down from time to time and is not available in certain areas – this could leave you lost and exposed without a secondary means. Keep maps and compasses in a map pouch for safe keeping. Laminated local and regional maps are recommended as well as a secondary compass to check the primary.

Rain gear such as a poncho and umbrella are common items that do not stand out when properly used. These items are easily stored in a pack and quickly deployed during inclement weather or when needing to mask body parts and features. Concealment adds a layer of privacy and a void of stimulation. Outside of active camouflage, brightly colored rain gear can be used to distract and source attention.

Sniper veils are handy to have in your bag just as an oversized bandana or shemagh. A sniper veil aids in concealment by acting as a camouflage cover when draped over the body when in hiding. Most sniper veils are a mesh-like construction – breathable, available in a medley of colors and patterns, and semitransparent.

Spare ammunition for your sidearm can be stored in your bag to keep surplus close at hand. Storing a firearm in the pack is not recommended unless you have complete control over it at all times. It is easier to maintain control over a firearm when it's on your person.

Spare batteries are much faster to use than waiting for your phone to charge. A spare battery at home, in your vehicle, and in your pack will expand your capabilities quickly and efficiently. Depending on the type of batteries you have, it makes sense to top them off on a regular basis to keep them in a state of readiness. Many phones have expanded capacity batteries available to give you longer run time. A spare USB battery bank and a portable solar charger is another option to store in your pack. This allows you to power a cell phone or other electronic device on the go. Compact options are available such as those provided by the Anker brand.

A backup phone and charger is an easy and smart way to deal with a lost, stolen, or broken primary phone. Disposable phones can be had at big box stores or online for cheap. Most throw away travel style phones do not require contracts, service is provided via a prepaid service card. Basic phones can be had for under $30 and can be stored in both your vehicle and pack. It would be advised to top off these phones weekly to ensure they have a charge when needed. It's a bonus when your backup phone uses the same charger as your primary phone.

Survival knives may sound excessive for an everyday carry bag, but they should be considered according to your needs. For those in an urban area this may not be so applicable, but for those commuting to or from rural areas it's worth a look. A survival style fixed blade gives you added capability to manipulate your environment which may greatly influence your options. The gray man is all about options and awareness! A survival knife could be used to help construct a shelter, make a fire, harvest and skin animals, provide protection from predators, and make other tools to make the situation easier to manage. If a traditional fixed blade survival knife isn't for you, look at full size multitools as another option. Leatherman and Victorinox have a few models that make ideal wilderness survival tools.

Multitools are handy to have available and there are many sizes to pick from. Those too large and bulky for everyday carry are good contenders for the bag. Take your time when selecting a multitool because there are many formats to choose from. Other tools that may be of interest to keep in the gray man everyday carry bag include a compact pry bar, bolt cuter, folding hand saw, sillcock key, and precision tweezers.

Water, water bottles, and water filters are desirable items to have with you in case access to potable water is limited. Keep your water bottles concealed when possible, those without water will possibly target those with during a crisis. A metal water bottle is more adaptable and capable than a plastic bottle, but the plastic container is easier to carry. Another option is to include a hydration bladder in your bag, this typically gives you more capability than a single bottle. There are downsides when using a bladder though, each user will have to decide what is best for them. An inline filter can be had for both bottles and bladders and are highly recommended.

Use these examples to build a foundation when constructing an everyday carry system. Always start with essential gear and add additional types if desired.

Gray Man Emergency Planning

"By failing to prepare, you are preparing to fail." – Benjamin Franklin

Formulate plans through research and discussion to maximize the use of your material assets, skills, knowledge and tactics. Being organized will aid you through this process. Set a timeline when certain planning is to be done, this will keep you and your group on the same schedule. One means to start your planning is to identify purposes, list your top 10 threats. Next determine goals and objectives. Order your plans with SMART objectives. SMART is an acronym for Specific, Measureable, Achievable, Relevant, and Time bound objectives. Have a primary, secondary, and backup strategy for each threat. An example list of identified threats could look like this:

#1 Home Invasion

#2 House Fire

#3 Major Trauma Injury

#4 Civil Unrest / Riots

#5 Getting Robbed at Gun Point

#6 Tornado

#7 Pandemic

#8 Hazardous Material Evacuation

#9 Loss of job

#10 Vehicle Breakdown

List resources to overcome each threat, this may include time, material assets, leverage, knowledge, skills, and tactics. List constraints of concern. Assign accountability to each plan. And finally list a detailed strategy outline highlighting specific actions.

After plans are made-up, organize resources into workable systems. Know how to get to egress locations from different areas you regularly frequent. Provide yourself with options to get there.

Review emergency plans with those in your inner circle. Write a procedure reference and keep it with your emergency kits. Review procedures on a regular basis, practice egress several times a year at different times of the day and week. Take note of the drills and examine the outcomes to better the procedure. Look at how each person reacts and how previous training and drills enhanced results.

Emergency planning should not just include local incidents but regional and national events too. Be mindful of how society is functioning and the delicate balance needed to ensure law and order. Study past events to better understand what is likely to happen in the future. The past repeats itself, those who know how humans react will be better equipped to handle what is before us.

Humans in power typically misuse or abuse their position for their own interest. We see this all throughout history, leaders of great power doing their will and not of the people. It therefore makes sense to be prepared for power struggles and conflict regardless of what country you live in. Political tensions historically have antagonized civil unrest and disrupted everyday living. Look to past natural and manmade disasters to see how they affect an area for months or even years. Earthquakes, hurricanes, and accidents involving toxic materials influence population centers within a host of factors. During most emergencies, if you have what you need avoid human contact. Desperate humans can be more of a threat that the disaster you are working through. The less contact with others the less opportunity to be taken advantage of or harmed.

Do you have plans? If not, are you working on solutions?

Gray Man Survival Kit

Unlike traditional survival kits a gray man needs enhanced cover options to blend in and disguise. The gray man also needs material resources to create opportunities, gain access into locations, and create distractions when needed. The gray man survival kit benefits from the following elements:

#1 Shelter /Cover: Provide yourself protection from the elements and from watchful eyes. Environmental camouflage should match the baseline norm of the area. Physical shelter options such as a tarp or tent should be considered. Include adaptable clothing and accessories to stay dry, warm and to alter your appearance. Have the means to look natural in your environment. Study a location to understand what is commonly found in it.

#2 Cordage: 50 to 100' of your preferred cordage makes for a medley of uses. Bankline, parachute cord, and Kevlar cordage are widely used due to versatility, compactness, and strength.

#3 Food & Water: Include a water bottle, filter, and food sack to hold your provisions. Stock your pack with enough food and water to get you through likely emergencies in your area. Rotate your water and food on a regular basis, this is especially important in warmer climates.

#4 Tools: Having the means to repair and build expands ones options in a survival situation. A survival knife, multitool, and folding hand saw is a solid starting point for your kit.

#5 Protection: Keeping yourself safe from threats is a wide topic to explore, but how are you planning to neutralize active threats set to harm you. Research and acquire the supplies and tools best to defend with. Preservation of life and health should be top priorities, therefore firearms may need to be included in your planning, training and kits.

#6 Fire: Making fire gives you the resource to create light, cook, create warming heat to maintain core body temperature, and to make tools. Have numerous means of making fire, several stored tinder options, and a means to secure these elements. A fire kit should be included in all survival kits.

#7 Signaling / Communications: Have several means to attract attention and relay information during an emergency. Signal mirrors, flares, whistles, small crank style emergency radios, and 2-way radios are possible options. Use shadows and natural contrasting elements to bring attention to your location if lost or injured.

#8 Navigation: Have several means to orient yourself for efficient travel and self-rescue. A map of your area, compass, backup compass, GPS, and a smart phone can be viable material assets to navigate with. In remote locations a satellite phone and transponder may be recommended. Learn shadow and star methods to orient yourself in the case you are separated from your gear.

#9 Medical: First aid skills and supplies are needed when preparing to respond to medical injuries. First aid and trauma supplies which make up your medical kit is a complex subject requiring thorough research. What you will need will be determined by the level of training you have received. Schedule skill building classes on a regular basis to stay current and to advance your medical skills. Effective medical training builds muscle memory which allows faster response to medical emergencies.

#10 Repair: Simple and common items can be helpful during an emergency and thus are desirable to store in your kit. Some repair items to consider include duct tape, cordage, super glue, silicon tubing, zip ties, wire, ranger bands of various sizes, patches, sewing kit, plastic bags, and safety pins.

#11 Illumination: Having a few light sources layered in your survival kit is highly recommended and extremely useful. When using disposable batteries select lights with the same battery type. This does three things – reduces complexity when storing spares, allows other devices to run off batteries in another device if no spares are available, and streamlines battery type when sourcing additional batteries. A LED headlamp makes an ideal primary light while a compact LED flashlight works well as a secondary option. Small flood lights such as a tent lantern is advisable as well as a keychain type light which stays on your person. Small LED lanterns typically have long run times and some are rechargeable with portable solar chargers. Selecting rechargeable headlamps and flashlights with USB charging ports is also an option when avoiding the use of disposable batteries. Light can be used to identify threats, disorient attackers, signal, communicate in code over distances, and travel or perform tasks in low light conditions.

#12 Trade & Access: Depending on the crisis barter and trade may be more desirable to some than the local currency. Keep a few items in your kit to barter and trade with. This may be needed to acquire to gear, food, or safe passage depending on the situation. Examples of barter and trade items include alcohol, tobacco products, antibiotics, batteries, compact radios, and lighters. Be careful not to make yourself a target when trading in hostile locations. Trading food and medical supplies may bring more attention to you than is desirable. Trading weapons and ammunition is not advised because it could be used against you and your group.

#13 Specialized Tools: Have tools to enhance your ability to overcome the challenges presented in your environment. Lock picks, pry bars, binoculars, and radios act like force multipliers - giving you an edge during worse case events. When possible select gear that has multiuse characteristics.

#14 Pack: A backpack is one of the most efficient means to carry supplies. It allows even distribution of weight on the shoulders, back, and hips. Select a pack after all contents has been acquired. You won't know what size of pack to get until you have all the contents. Select a low profile backpack in neutral colors – you want to look ordinary and non-tactical. Day packs or smaller hiking packs make good options.

Have resupplies at your egress locations. Your survival kit is limited in what it contains, additional resources should be stored to continue self-preservation. Common items to store in a cache at the egress location include additional food, water, medical supplies, tools, cash, firearms, ammunition, clothing, blankets, and batteries.

Gray Man Transportation

Transportation is essential if you are to be mobile in your community. While there are those who may be able to walk to all desired destinations, most will need one or more means to get there. For those in an urban setting a bicycle, skate board, or public transportation may be all you need on a regular basis. But what about during a disaster? Will public transportation be functioning then?

It's beneficial to have your own transportation during an emergency. You may not be able to rely on anyone thus the need for options. Having your own vehicle(s) enhances your ability to move freely about on demand. Public transportation is useful during ordinary times but the dependency is a major drawback. Those in suburban and rural locations may not have options that are afforded to those in urban landscapes. It's therefore a need to have a vehicle. When selecting a transport option consider common ordinary vehicles, but beware of the commonly stolen makes and models.

At the time of writing (2018) the most commonly stolen cars included (make, model & year):

#1 Honda Accord (1997)

#2 Honda Civic (1998)

#3 Ford F-Series Pickup (2006)

#4 Chevrolet Silverado Pickup (2004)

#5 Toyota Camry (2016)

#6 Nissan Altima (2015)

#7 Ram Pickup (2001)

#8 Toyota Corolla (2015)

#9 Chevrolet Impala (2008)

#10 Jeep Cherokee / Grand Cherokee (2000)

When selecting a vehicle be mindful of color and any other feature that causes it to look unique, custom, or premium. Limit your colors to those more muted and avoid models with chromed features. Wheels should not stand out as well as any other feature that creates contrast. If one is avoiding attention do not add vanity plates or custom window decals. Bumper stickers are not recommended either. A bumper sticker advertising your church may seem harmless, but it informs others with mal-intent. One can infer from a simple church bumper sticker that you leave at some point to go to church, you believe in god, and the name of the church you attend. Service times can be looked up, and through deduction and observation one could learn when you leave home for church service. This allows criminals a window of opportunity to take advantage of. Don't freely give out information that can be used against you.

Don't draw attention to yourself by playing your high-end car stereo so loud others can hear it. Keep vehicle clean but not so much that people notice it. Try not to look stealthy by blacking out your vehicle. Tinted windows are ok, but make sure they are legal and do not create contrast with your vehicle. Don't use aftermarket mufflers to make vehicle sound loud or unique. Keep vehicle as factory as possible, do not customize your vehicle. If getting a passenger car look for one that offers space to conceal gear. If your vehicle does not have a trunk, create a concealed space not visible from the outside. To enhance privacy when buying a van, select one with fewer windows. Off road vehicles typically attract attention unless they are commonly used in the local area. Do not install rows of flood lights, aftermarket bumpers, roll bars, tow winch, and air horns – they attract attention.

It's advised to keep phone numbers of a wrecker service, and several alternative means of transportation in your phone and wallet. Keep your vehicle maintained and serviced when needed. Secure the vehicle and items in the vehicle when not in use. Do not leave items in the vehicle that would tempt a criminal. Avoid crimes of opportunity by not storing your keys in your vehicle and keeping all items out of sight. A vehicle lock box or safe is recommended to secure valuables or firearms when traveling. Locations to mount a lock box or safe could include under a seat, in the trunk, or on the floorboard. Mounting options will vary from vehicle to vehicle.

Car alarms, motion sensors, vehicle trackers, and camera surveillance are all options which can be low profile but provide a level of security. In being prudent, it makes sense to protect your ride, but don't go overboard - it will attract attention.

When buying a vehicle it makes sense to buy used and not new. Unless you are flush with cash, it's not advisable to pay the mark up to be the first owner. Most new modern vehicles are not investments but a liability. They depreciate in value over time, they require maintenance to be road worthy, and property tax and insurance has to be paid to remain legal. Vehicles may be a hobby, but if you're the majority, it's simply a means to get from place to place efficiently and safely.

Modern technology has made it possible to get affordable vehicles that are reliable and cost efficient. If all you need is a commuter vehicle look to the many high efficiency options that get over 35 mph. Kia, Hyundai, Honda, Ford, and Toyota continue to elevate quality year to year and are high value options. When researching your next vehicle, look at the lifetime ownership cost to determine in part what best fits your budget.

Your vehicle can be used not only for transportation but as a shelter and mobile base. While this is referred to as car camping, the gray man adds the element of covertness. This practice is called stealth camping or road ghosting. Stealth camping is camping or dwelling at a location without being noticed or suspected of occupying your vehicle. To the outsider your parked vehicle looks unoccupied and unremarkable. You can potentially stealth camp anywhere within reason. This includes urban, industrial (parkways), suburban, and rural locales. While in theory you can use most vehicles to do this, some are clearly more effective than others. Mid to full size SUV's and cargo vans tend to work best. Passenger vans can be converted as well as large wagon style cars. Passenger vehicles with flat folding seats are highly preferred over those which have to be removed. A flat surface is desirable to form a (cargo) storage and sleeping space. In my opinion the Ford Explorer makes a great stealth camper option for one to two people. Smaller cargo vans and trucks with low profile toppers work well too. Just avoid the larger traditional truck campers, they don't play into your objective. The flat laying seats on the Ford Explorer allow the second and third rows to be used as a living quarters. You can setup a bed roll directly on the floor or build a platform to sleep on. A platform can allow you additional storage space and organization with the use of totes. A platform can be as simple as a piece of plywood cut to the interior space with added legs. If you have advanced carpentry skills you may want to install drawers instead of using totes under the raised platform. The following suggestions will help make your stealth camping experience more comfortable:

1. Have a means to heat and cool, this includes bringing appropriate clothing, blankets and bedding, portable heater, and fan.

2. Have an external power source, this could be as simple as a portable power supply and solar charger.

3. Have enough food and water, a storage of two gallons of water per person per day (minimum amount) and easy to prepare foods is a simple approach to follow. Water storage can easily be done with a couple of 5 gallon water jugs with spigots. Foods which require no cooking is recommended, but for those needing a stove consider a single burner camp stove. A gas fueled camp stove is stealthier than making a camp fire. Don't forget any kitchen utensils.

4. Have a hygiene kit, store wet wipes, towels, soap, toothbrush, toothpaste, and hand sanitizer to keep healthy and clean.

5. Have the means to illuminate your environment, a headlamp and compact lantern will satisfy most needs.

6. Have a radio and cell phone to receive information and to communicate with others. For those avoiding tracking technology, keep the cell phone off with the battery out or store the phone in a faraday container.

7. Have basic repair tools, this will be useful for vehicle or gear repair. Consider storing a jumper kit, tow rope, engine oil, coolant, spare tire, jack, air compressor, tire plug kit, duct tape, and road hazard reflectors.

8. Have local and regional maps for reference when looking for a detour route or a location to stealth camp.

9. Know which stores in your area are open 24 hours, this allows you to seek shelter in the event you need more than your vehicle can provide.

10. Have a means to relieve yourself in an emergency. A small bucket with trash liner and sawdust can be used to deal with this need.

11. Have a means to protect yourself and those with you.

12. Have a means to shield your eyes and ears from excessive light and sound if stealth camping in urban or industrial parkways. Earplugs and an eye mask allow you to sleep during the day or in well-lit and noisy areas.

13. Have a means to be notified of potential threats outside your vehicle. One way to deal with this issue is to set up motion sensors around the outside of the vehicle. This may not be practical in high traffic locations.

14. Have blackout curtains so you can sleep during the day or have privacy when needed. Use Velcro strips to make it easy to attach and remove fabric panels.

15. Have a tarp to create a vehicle shade extension when parking in remote unpopulated locations. Remember – don't park at the same spot each night. Even when staying at the same location, it's best to move around just in case you are being watched. This does two things. First, it shows that you are not settling in and secondly it makes a statement that you are active. People tend to avoid confrontation with active people more so than those who are passive.

If a personal vehicle is not appropriate for you then look to see how to maximize other modes of transportation. When using public transport such as trains, planes, trams, trolleys, buses, ferries, and taxi services be safety conscious. When possible sit near an exit and have a backup plan to get to your destination if the primary fails. Sit near the front of the vehicle to communicate with the operator in case of an emergency. Notice the emergency features of the vehicle when you board. Always let others know when and where you are going when traveling alone.

Gray Man Communications

"The most important thing in communication is hearing what isn't said." – Peter Drucker

Communications is a diverse topic, it involves both technology and human interaction.

The first thing you can do is learn how to operate modern communication technology. This includes smart phones, tablets, and how to navigate on a desktop and or laptop. Next, look at how you communicate with others. Be mindful of what you say, where your say it, and how you say it. Many times problems arise because of misunderstandings. Always be clear and concise in what you are saying.

It's best not to tell others sensitive information such as personal identifying material. If you're a prepper that too should be kept private. Discuss topics that are common in your community when having a conversation with outsiders. An outsider is anyone which is outside of your inner group. The inner group typically contains certain family members and trusted friends. Those who use gray man tactics tends to coincide with prepared minded people, therefore it's not uncommon for the gray man to be a prepper. Preppers are not socially accepted by mainstream standards, by most estimates they make up less than 5% of the population. They are hard to know because most live unassuming lifestyles. It's advised never to advertise if you're a prepper or survivalist. It's also important to keep confidential information to yourself if you know of others that are preppers. Practice OPSEC (operational security) every day.

Safety & security should be a top priority as part of your OPSEC. The use of encryption and VPN (virtual private network) on your computers is highly recommended. Don't use public computers and Wi-Fi without updated firewalls and malware software. Public internet connections are not secure networks. A VPN extends a private network across a public network to send and receive data with enhanced security and privacy. Mozilla Firefox is safer than Internet Explorer, Microsoft Edge and Google Chrome. Delete cookies regularly from your phone and computers. You can disable the use of cookies on your browser. If disabling cookies denies access to trusted sites, white list them and block all others. Don't use the "remember me" function on websites. Avoid using social media sites. Delete social media accounts when possible. If you use social media such as YouTube, Instagram, Facebook, or Google+ don't post private information. Always use privacy settings when possible. Use StartPage or Duck-Duck-Go search engines, they are safer and more private than Google, Yahoo, or Bing. Be aware that most email services monitor your correspondence, collect information and sell them to others. Always assume all internet traffic including emails and site history is monitored, logged, and stored. Never give out passwords to anyone. Don't go to unknown sites or click on suspicious emails. Keep all software up-to-date including antivirus and firewall protections.

When receiving physical mail consider using a UPS store address, this keeps packages from being shipped to your house. You can list your driver's license and car registration to a UPS address. You can also use an LLC or a Trust to buy a house and have your LLC address be your P.O. Box or UPS store address. By not identifying or listing your physical address you limit access from others. This limits scams and junk mail. Mail at a P.O. Box or UPS store address is more secure and creates less attention than a residential address.

For additional privacy list your phone number(s) in the National Do Not Call Registry at 1-888-382-1222. Here are a few other ways to increase your privacy and safety: obtain a private unlisted number, use a no contract service plan, turn off or delete apps with tracking features, turn off location feature, use security features to deny access from unauthorized users, be aware that cloud storage is not always private nor secure, be aware of how social media sites track, record, and use your information, and limit phone use in public spaces where others may hear your conversation or hack into your device.

When it comes to human relations make friends with those you contact frequently. Don't make enemies when possible, it's just one more element to deal with. The more allies you have the better. Get to know those who you interact with in your community, let them share thoughts and news to update you on local issues. It's amazing how just a handful of well-connected people can inform you on important local matters. These contacts contribute to your diverse pool of resources, it's called HUMINT (human intelligence). HUMINT is like having boots on the ground, eyes behind your head. Use your relationships within your community to gather and source information to increase awareness of your environment.

Communication also involves covert coded means. The efficient use of letters, words, sounds, images, or gestures can be used to communicate to another quickly and privately. Use shortened words over longer ones, length and pronounceability are a big part in effective coded communication.

Gray Man Specialized Gear

Here are recommendations of gear to consider adding to kits or locations for specialized needs and uses:

Balaclava face mask

Binoculars

Body armor – both ballistic and blunt force trauma soft body armor

Bug detector / RF scanner

Collapsible carbine

Concealed carry firearm with sound suppressor

Concealed cutting tools – neck, ankle, inside waistband blades

Covert backpacks and sling packs

Covert tactical clothing

Dyneema puncture resistant gloves

Enhancement sound detection gear

Face paint

IFAK – individual first aid kit / trauma kit

Impact resistant eyewear

Low output red / blue lights

Night vision

Radio scanner

Sniper veil

Thermal optics

Voice Scrambler

Wig & other disguises

Gray Man Skills

Use common activities such as camping, fishing, hunting, trapping, cooking, budgeting, sports, and hobbies to build skills and confidence individually and within family groups. By using socially accepted activities you avoid suspicion but grow in practical knowledge. Some skills should only be practiced at home or in private spaces. Lock picking is one example of a skill that is frowned on because people are vulnerable to it. People tend to be fearful of what they don't understand. Through awareness, the gray man seeks to expand available options for an end goal of efficient problem solving. Practice your skills regularly to maintain muscle memory.

Small kids talk so don't tell your kids about being gray or that you're a prepper, survivalist or anything else that is controversial. When your kids get older and understand the importance of keeping certain topics confidential, slowly make them aware.

Here are a few examples of basic gray man skills to learn and practice: camouflage, cooking, fire making, gear repair, hunting, trapping, fishing, foraging, information gathering, knife sharpening, knot making, lock picking, medical training for minor and major injuries, navigation, water purification, self-defense, sewing, shelter building, signaling, stealth camping, stealth movement, tool making, and torch making.

Gray Groups

Most gray people do not gather in large groups but tend to stay with either family or move about alone. In groups you have the opportunity to share information, socialize, work on projects collectively, and share interest with others. Prepper groups are one option when looking for like-minded people. Just remember that not all preppers can be gray.

Outside of personal gatherings what about how to use public groups? One way to use a public gathering is for cover, get lost in the crowd by flowing with it - act like everyone else. Say what others are saying, act surprised when other do. Don't look overly confident in large groups because you stand out. The only reason that you would look overly confident is if you were the group leader or someone that opposes the group. It's about how you handle yourself, how you look and act.

It's less noticeable to follow a crowd to get past it than trying to walk through it at an angle. Exit from crowds by moving with smaller side groups. Stay close enough to look like you're with others, but not so close that those nearby notice you. People perceived as being alone look weaker than those in a group, this makes them more vulnerable to the criminal element. Personal space is typically a bubble 3 to 4 feet from you, social space is typically 4 to 12 feet. Public space is 12 or more feet. These are a rough estimate for those in most societies. Some have larger and others smaller bubbles. In groups or a crowd of people, it's common to be in very close contact – sometimes even touching. In these situations it may be best to work to the outer edge (of the group) to better control distance from others. The more space you have from others the better the reaction time in a self-defense scenario.

Adapt and improvise as you enter different environments and interact with different people. It's smart not to walk next to the same group for an extended amount of time. By being near but not a part of the group you will eventually be noticed.

Gray Man Off Grid

Do you have what you need to function off grid?

The electrical grid is usually the first thing thought off when the grid is mentioned. But what about other grids such as communication networks, natural gas utilities, sewer systems, water works, and trash services. Do you have the means to function efficiently if these services ceased to function? Let's look at each of these individually and provide an alternative.

It's easy to feel vulnerable and helpless when the power is out, most of us rely on electricity in some capacity. So how could you deal with a sudden electrical grid outage? One way is to have a means to generate your own electricity. This could be in the form of a gas powered generator, wind turbine, or solar collector. Store extra batteries (both disposable and rechargeable) for commonly used devices, include applicable adaptors for all devices to allow for interfacing with various power sources. Power sources may require the use of an AC jack, DC plug, and direct wiring from a solar, hand crank or gas generator. Hand crank radios and lights are handy during a power outage, while a portable solar collector can charge battery banks and essential devices. A residential solar system is recommended, but they don't have to cost big money. A few 100 watt panels and a handful of deep cycle batteries (such as 12 volt golf cart batteries) can provide much relief during an extended outage. Your solar system could be permanently mounted on a structure or kept stored until needed.

When communications fail we are disconnected from the world. It's thus important to retain several communication resources to keep contact with others and to source information. Common forms of communication are through cellular networks, landlines, satellite systems, fiber optics, microwave relays, and radio transmissions such as AM, FM, NOAA weather, and shortwave. Many of us rely on our cell phones to call, text, email, interact with social media, surf the web, and conduct business online. We are more dependent on technology than ever before. So how do we deal with communication blackouts? One resource option is to build a personal library of reference material. This makes for times the internet is not available more manageable. It's also advisable to keep several emergency style radios for monitoring local news, weather, and civil emergency alerts. If radio traffic fails to provide needed information, use local contacts to source additional information. Have a plan to meet with others at a certain location and time if traditional communications are not usable. Ham (amateur) radio gear could be added to extend the communication capability of any group. Have set frequencies and times of use to organize communication schedules. In hostile environments you will want to limit radio traffic and use coded messages.

Natural gas, propane, and butane, are relied on by many households to warm living spaces, cook food, and provide light. Luckily many homes have storage tanks and do not rely solely on piped in gas. For those who do not have stored gas, a backup tank would be helpful during interruptions.

Sewers are one of the most underappreciated services in urban living. The ability to manage waste is critical to community health, what would you do with your human waste without it? One option is a dry toilet. This includes the composting toilet, urine-diverting dry toilet, arborloo, container-based toilet, bucket toilet, and pit latrines. One of the simplest is the bucket toilet which can be made from a common 5 gallon bucket, lid, foam pool noodle float, garbage bags, and absorbing material such as sand, cat litter with silica gel, saw dust, wood chips, and newspaper. Place a garbage bag in the bucket to form a liner. Take your foam pool noodle and cut off a length the circumference of the mouth of the bucket. Create a slit on one side of the float to allow it to slip onto the lip of the bucket. The float will help to secure the liner and double as a seat cushion. Insert filler medium of choice into the bag to absorb waste products and odors. After use add additional absorbing material and remove seat cushion. Tie off bag if needed and discard when bucket is half full. Secure the lid on the bucket when not in use. Store extra fill material and bags alongside with your container-based dry toilet.

Potable water is an essential need and thus needs to be available when it stops flowing into your house. The easiest way to have extra water is to store it in water jugs. Other approaches include water cisterns, wells, ponds, lakes, rivers, pools, and rain catchment systems. If you have no gutters to divert rain into a rain barrel use a depression in your yard. You can create a depression by digging a hole and lining it with plastic sheeting or a water tight tarp. Dig your rain catchment depression in a low elevation area. Protect outdoor water sources by covering them with plastic sheeting or tarps, this reduces loss from evaporation when the sun is out.

Trash removal is something most take for granted. You set your trash out on certain days and people arrive and take it away. Without this service hygiene and sanitation would become a more difficult issue. How would you manage your garbage if no outside service was available? Common methods of disposal outside of garbage pickup include burning, burial and recycling. Recycle by repurposing materials to solve current needs. Don't forget to compost food scraps to make rich soil for your gardens.

Manipulation

"When it comes to controlling human beings, there is no better instrument than lies. Because you see, humans live by beliefs. And beliefs can be manipulated. The power to manipulate beliefs is the only thing that counts." – Michael Ende

People manipulate others to get what they want, this is a fact of life. Manipulation can be used for the betterment of others or to take advantage of them. Being able to identify when others are manipulating helps to protect against getting taken advantage of. Manipulation involves mastering emotions – expressions have to be believable. Acting classes are sometimes used to help develop mastery in projecting emotional states. Debate and speaking classes will help in the development of persuasion skills. These skills are based in logic and reasoning and requires practice for refinement. The organization and presentation of emotions, thoughts, and words are essential to convincing others to yield to a request.

Manipulation is more effective when similarities are established between all parties. Mirroring can be used to develop rapport, this is done by copying body language, words, and emotions. Mirroring is a method sometimes referred to as pacing. Pacing is used to create connections which provide an "in", this typically starts with unconscious cues which result in a sense of ease.

Using a display of emotions may not be effective or appropriate with certain people or in some environments. In these cases a calm and persuasive method is more beneficial. The use of charisma, humor, politeness, helpfulness, and sincerity helps to make others feel special. This is important because people love to feel special. In this state people are more receptive to doing something for another.

Eye contact helps build rapport just as asking about how one feels. Personal or occupational interests can be an entry point when giving attention. People typically respond positively to constructive attention and sincere compliments. People also enjoy when they feel cared for and loved, this too is sometimes exploited during manipulation. The practice of confidence can be a powerful tool when mixed with pride. If a person takes themselves seriously others will too.

Manipulation techniques are developed over time with practice. Many learn manipulation from watching others and from repeated attempts. The ability to read people helps in understanding what motivates them. Every person has a different emotional and psychological makeup. Because every person is different they too have different motivators. Some people are more susceptible to emotional responses while others require logic and facts. Manipulators often use guilt to exploit those in unique situations and status. A number of people are chiefly motivated by comfort and certainty, while others desire variety and excitement. Significance motivates some just as love, connection, and personal growth. Many people are motivated to serve others, and it's this need to contribute that makes them vulnerable. Giving people are easier to take advantage of than someone who is guarded and unreceptive.

The following are proven tactics used in manipulation.

#1 *Use of an unreasonable request followed by a more reasonable one.* A manipulator benefits from the contrast between the two requests. Most people are more compliant after hearing the second request because it's not as extreme as the first. Example – "Can I have $30 for a taxi?" Follow up – "Can I have a $1 for the city bus?"

#2 *Use of an unusual request before the real request.* Example – "Could you (stranger) hold the door for me as I move supplies in?" Follow up – "Thanks so much for your help, would it be too much trouble to get a quick ride with you to get lunch?" People are more apt to give or help if they have a connection with those asking.

#3 *Use of fear, then relief.* Start the request with the entertainment of worry and fear by stating negative outcomes. After the initial build up relief is provided with good news - they are told they are not affected by the issue. Example – "Normally this make and model would need a new engine after this many miles." Follow up – Luckily for you, we can do a simple and cost effective engine flush to solve your issues. Would you like the engine flush?" This tactic allows a party to let their guard down because they believe the situation could have been worse. Allowing others to feel hopeful and lucky can be beneficial to a manipulator.

#4 *Use of the guilt complex.* Those with a guilt complex can be identified and exploited. Example – A well-dressed man walking into church is approached by a weathered lady asking for food. The man is put on the spot in front of others and feels an obligation to help or look hypocritical to his beliefs. Most people avoid negative attention and will act in order to keep a clear conscious free from regret and guilt. The request for food would make most people feel guilty. This is especially true if the party in question obviously has the outward means to solve this trivial issue.

#5 *Use of bribery with blackmail or rewards.* Example – "Drive me to get groceries or I will tell your neighbor you stole their garden hose." Bribery works better when it's disguised as a compromise, the more subtle the better. Example – "I'll wash your car if you drive me to the mall."

#6 *Play the role of the victim.* Playing the role of the victim gains sympathy from most people. The more simple-minded and innocent a person plays the more effective. It helps to act pathetic and depressed to be more believable. Guilt is commonly used when playing the victim role to magnify results. Example – "I'm jobless and homeless, I see you drive a nice car, could I please have a few dollars for food sir?"

#7 *Use logic with rational minded people.* Build your case for why you should get your request. Use three or more result oriented reasons why the thing you want would benefit you and the other party. Find common ground and bring conclusions full circle - how what you are asking is best for everyone. When dealing with rational minded people it's important to stay calm and present your case. Leave emotions out of your interactions. Example – "If you help me get my lawn mower fixed I will be able to cut my yard and help you with yours. By keeping our yards cut we reduce the number of snakes which may harm our children. It also goes without saying that a well-kept yard looks appealing and is something to be proud of."

Additional techniques manipulators use:

Successful manipulation of others benefit from consistency – they stay in character.

Manipulators use past favors to manipulate those close to them. They remind them of things they have done for them in the past. They use the past to motivate them in the present. They use emotions when needed. Manipulators will even remind them of times when they let them down.

Manipulators use sex appeal. They create sexual tension to get others to do what they want.

Crying in public. It's effective with certain people, the key is being believable.

Manipulators play off their wants as a compromise. If you do this I will do that.

Manipulators downplay the importance of their request. They are on their best behavior. They build up to asking a favor after having helped the party being manipulated.

Manipulators ask people for favors when caught off guard. People are less likely to say no or disagree at the end of a long day.

Disappearing

"Be slow in choosing a friend, slower in changing."
– Benjamin Franklin

A traditional definition of a gray man involves blending into an environment – becoming invisible to those around you, but sometimes you need to disappear. Disappearing in the true sense is starting over, literally starting a new life. This is not for everyone and requires much planning and strategy. For most, disappearing will never be more than a mind exercise. But for those who really need to start over here's some information to consider.

Preparation is key, it takes time to evolve solutions and create a new life profile. It's vital to know exactly who or what you're disappearing from. Is it a government, a criminal element, or people you just want to break ties with? Know the legal ramifications of disappearing, how you disappear makes a difference in the eyes of the law. In most locations it's lawful to disappear, but you can't legally fake your death or assume another person's identity. Stealing someone's identity is not only illegal but potentially dangerous for you. People have hidden dark secrets, a person who looks like a model citizen may have a long criminal record and outstanding warrants. Always think through your planning to make sure the solutions are viable.

One of the first things you want to do is distance yourself from others. Slowly start to spend less time with those you normally socialize with. Cutting social ties is essential to leaving behind your old life and starting a new one. This process most likely will be painful, but if the objective is to start over certain things must be done. Excuses may have to be made with others to start this process.

Disappearing is much easier alone than with others. It's difficult enough to disappear as an individual, the dedication and time required to be successful can be overwhelming. If you have pets, adopt them out to others that would take care of them. Social media accounts need to be used less and less. Eventually you need to close the accounts. Getting off social media is important to minimize the presence of your old life. Closing social media accounts such as Facebook, Twitter,

YouTube, and Instagram is just the beginning. You also want to close out email and online banking accounts as well.

Withdraw money from your banking and retirement accounts in a manner that would not attract attention. If a bank asks about the increase in withdrawals give them a believable but boring answer. As you withdraw resources slow the use of credit and debit card use. After accounts have been liquidated cancel all cards and put a freeze on your credit. This should be done with each of the three main credit reporting agencies - Experian, Equifax, & TransUnion. Destroy your cards and get used to using cash for everything. Save as much money as you can before disappearing, starting over is not cheap.

In most cases it would strategically be best to quit your job just before you disappear. Doing this eliminates attention from those that might start looking for you if you abruptly stopped showing up for work. It also benefits you to pay off all debts, taxes, and not be in a lease at the time of disappearing. If in a lease it would be a good idea to pay a few months in advance before disappearing. This will lessen any tension with the landlord when they discover you moved out.

At some point before disappearing you will need to gather all identification and photos, both digital and physical. A determination will need to be made what to do with them. Should you keep them and store them in a safe location, or do you destroy all evidence of the life you're leaving behind? Leaving behind images could aid in finding you at a later date. Avoid new pictures as you transition into your new life.

The stuff at your residence will need to be sold or donated. Do this a little at a time in local yard sales and consignment shops. Also consider donating items that are harder to sell to local charity organizations. As a last resort take items that will not sell or be accepted as a donation to your local dump. By getting rid of items from your old life you clear the path for the new one. Having items from the past can give clues to others that might be looking for you.

Shortly before disappearing cancel your mobile phone service and acquire a cheap burner phone. Use phone services which require no identification, no service contract, and which can be reloaded via prepaid cards. Select a well-known service provider to make finding prepaid cards less of a hassle.

When selecting a new name do not use one that starts with the same letter as your current one. Avoid similar sounding names or nicknames. If you're a writer don't use a name from one of your characters. Don't pick a name that is exotic or attention getting. An ordinary name is best. Common male names include James, John, Robert, Michael, William, David, Richard, Joseph, Thomas, and Charles. Common female names include Mary, Patricia, Jennifer, Linda, Elizabeth, Barbara, Susan, Jessica, Sarah, and Margaret. According to the Social Security Administration, these were the top ten names for each gender over the last 100 years.

Some people opt to legally change their name. While an option, it can be traceable by determined individuals. Another option is to buy, manufacture, or manipulate identification. This is obviously illegal, I do not condone illegal activity but it is an option for those in dire life threatening danger. One unlawful technique is to request a birth certificate of a deceased infant that was born about the same time as you. This will take some research but people do use this to gain access to other forms of identification such as a driver's license and social security card. Identification in developed countries is sometimes required when traveling and when buying certain goods. Operating a vehicle, flying in a commercial plane, and buying tobacco and alcohol products require identification.

Take time to sort out transportation issues when you disappear. It's necessary to get rid of any vehicles before disappearing. Keeping the same vehicle makes it too easy for someone to locate you, all they would have to do is a VIN search.

Where are you going to go when you first disappear? In some ways it's easier to disappear in a large crowded busy city than an isolated rural location. This is not to say that you couldn't pull off a rural relocation, but it makes more sense for most to start the transition in a larger heavily populated city. If you have identification then renting will be easier than without. Consider renting a room in a house, many offer privacy and are affordable. Be prepared to pay a few months of rent as a retainer or security deposit. After a few months or whatever time you feel is appropriate - move to another location to create more distance from your past life. Make it more difficult for someone to track you by moving several time before settling in at a location.

It's important to start a new employment history before your financial resources are expended. If you have ample resources it still would be advised to get a job to have a means to meet new people and integrate into your new environment. A simple part time job could strengthen your social contacts and help make allies at your new location. Be open to jobs you would not have previously considered. To jumpstart your work history manual labor and other undesirable jobs might be all that is available. Your job potential in part is dependent by the type of identification you can present. After securing a job keep a low profile and don't bring attention to yourself. Even when the job is not challenging, pretend to work hard and conceal your intelligence. Talk about what others talk about at work - don't stand out.

It's recommended to change your appearance for a fresh new look. Wear comfortable articles of clothing you would typically not wear. Always dress your age and try not to look younger or older. Get outside of your comfort zone and explore a different side of yourself. It may help to think of yourself as an actor playing a part.

Besides clothing changes you might want to dye your hair. Dye your hair a natural color to avoid attention. Wear a different type of brimmed hat than you normally would wear. This serves to change your look, to shield your facial features from on looking overhead cameras, and to change or conceal the facial profile.

Develop new mannerisms to mask older ones. Mannerisms can give a person away from a distance, always be mindful of them. Notice how you talk and what you say. The goal is to make a stranger of yourself, but not make yourself look strange. Make changes that allow you to blend in and mask your old identity. Keep a low profile when possible and act as others do. Redefine the norm by those around you.

As you develop the new you, challenge your new profile to improve it. Practice your new mannerisms, get comfortable in character, intuitively known your new likes and dislikes, and enjoy new hobbies. The old you needs to disappear so the development of a new character profile can take shape. Craft a history to go along with your character so that talking to others sounds natural. Here are some questions to practice with:

Where did you come from?

Where is your family?

What did you do before coming here?

Favorite food?

Favorite hobbies?

Favorite sport?

Favorite author?

Favorite music?

It's ok to make new friends with the locals, neighbors, and to be polite and civil to those in authority positions. Having others on your side will create allies, we can never have too many of those. An ally can be a roadblock to those looking for you. Allies can be an alibi to your new identity and be of great benefit as a social resource to alert you of potential danger. An alibi will confirm your new name and profile history to others, this in turn helps building a new active history. Always be consistent in the information you share with others. All stories should match. Don't be tempted to fall back into old habits, this can happen when we start to get comfortable and let our guard down. Never contact anyone from your past life, if you don't think you can handle this then disappearing is not for you.

Having people not looking for you is much preferred to when they are. If you have people looking be mindful not to let any new success become overtly public. If starting a new job or business consider minimizing your level of success for the first few years. There is nothing wrong with success or being recognized for accomplishments, but too much brings attention to yourself. Give yourself time when you first transition into your new life. Stay under the radar but don't be confined and limited by your exile.

Traveling can be tricky without being detected. Cameras are everywhere, this is especially true in larger cities. Video surveillance should play a factor in how you travel, this is especially true if others are looking for you. If you can walk or ride a bicycle to get where you need to go, it will simplify your life and be more affordable. Walking and operating a bicycle does not require identification, registration, insurance, and the issues of storing and maintaining a vehicle. From a gray man approach most bus, tram, and railway services would be preferred over air travel, taxi services, and hitchhiking. You want to minimize exposure but be in a position with maximum control. For example, if you're traveling in a taxi and it has an accident, you will surely have attention from the police at some point. It's best to be around more people so that you stand out less if an incident occurs.

Generally speaking it's easier to disappear the further you travel from your old life. Many people choose to disappear in other countries. Consider countries that you native in and know the language. For example, if you're a tall white male you would contrast if everyone around you is shorter and of a much darker skin color. South America is an ideal location for some because many areas are still developing and identification requirements are more relaxed. But for most people it's more practical to start over in a different part of their country. In the United States (for example) there are many different geographical and cultural havens to choose from. Many large cities in the US have ethnic specific areas to make it even easier to blend in. You can also (for example) select from coastal, mountain, desert, or tropical settings depending on what type of environment you wish to transition to. You have options, just go to a place that others would not expect you to be. Don't go to any location you have previously been to or have talked about before.

It may be helpful to use disinformation to cover your tracks. Before you disappear you may want to leave false clues of where you're going. This could include the use of false leads in stored computer files, social media links, emails, or computer browser. A road atlas could be left behind with a false destination circled and notes next to it. So if you're going to Texas then Maine or Canada could be a logical distraction point.

If going to nature is part of your initial life reset - you have a rough road ahead of you. Most people should not attempt this and would fail to endure. Depending on where and how long you plan to be out in nature, be sure to bring everything you need. List all necessities like a tent, portable stove, sleeping bag, warm clothes, water filter, and plenty of food. If you're going to commit to this approach, travel to a remote area away from prying eyes. Don't settle in a high traffic park or near the outskirts of a city. Research has shown that by staying clean and organized you keep your morale up. Having self-confidence and motivation is important during a difficult time like this.

Don't use physical mail for personal correspondence after you relocate. If needing to correspond with a third party use generic email accounts not linked to your old name. Use a P.O. Box or USPS store address to receive packages and bills.

Here is a story reported as being true, this is one example of a person disappearing:

"Everyone who I knew before 9/11 thinks I am dead. I changed my whole identity because I couldn't stand my life. Little back story first. My parents are very rich, my dad is a surgeon and mom owns a very expensive clothing store. I got married at 24, right after I finished my senior year at Brown, we lived pretty happily for a while, then I went to Law school and the whole thing started to crumble.

I was studying a lot, extremely busy and never had time to go home, so I guess it was partially my fault. As the years passed, my wife and I started to drift apart, wife stopped talking to me about her personal stuff, but we still made small talk about the news, neighbors, and stuff. But when I asked about her issues I was always met with, "Everything is fine honey."

Then, suddenly we had a baby and I thought everything would get better, but it only made it worse. My wife started accusing me of cheating on her. Our relationship went downhill very fast. Meanwhile, my parents stopped talking to me. My dad said I wasn't living up to his expectations and my mom took his side. Basically, my life was crap.

In the last 5 to 6 months before 9/11 my life became a routine that I just needed to do. Every day became harder to wake up. Then, a few weeks before 9/11 I discovered my wife had been cheating on me for the last 7 years and our 6 year old daughter wasn't mine. I didn't know what to do, I was seriously lost.

Then 9/11 happened.

My firm was located in the North building. I was at a client's house looking over some files when I heard the news. At first I freaked out, naturally. My coworkers and friends were in that building. Then it dawned on me everyone probably thinks I'm dead. I was standing there and thinking the same thing over and over again, and every time I thought it I felt such a weight off my shoulders, such a relief.

I took a cab to Garden City and just went into a bar, sipped beer while watching the news, stayed there until it closed. I was about to go home when I had a thought: "Why should I go home? I'm dead!"

I took a bus to a small town near Niagara Falls. My parents had a small house there that they never stayed at. I spent the night there, then went to the bank and took out all my savings from my personal account (about 80k).

I went to Canada.

I now live in a small RV park in Ontario. I changed my name and my appearance. I live a very modest life and couldn't be happier. Every year on 9/10, I go to the bar, tip the bartender $100, visit ground zero, and take a quick peek at the place where my ex-wife lives with her new husband. I always imagine going up to the door and knocking, telling her it's me, and seeing the look of shock on her face, but I never do."

-Anonymous

While this story certainly takes advantage of a circumstance, a better planned approach is advised. The more loose ends you leave the less likely success of disappearing. In this example, the wife may have welcomed the potential for tragedy, and not went looking for confirmation of death. Every situation presents different options, the choices you make determine in great part your outcomes. Disappearing isn't as simple as it sounds or looks.

Surveillance

The word surveillance comes from a French phrase for "watching over". Surveillance is made up of many methods depending on objectives, time, and available resources. The classic means to investigate and gather information is to follow and document routines and activities. Over time technology yielded more efficient means and the use of those became of great value. Some examples of modern surveillance include the use of closed circuit television (CCTV) cameras, finger prints, and DNA. Closed circuit television cameras are categorized as a form of preconstructive surveillance while finger prints and DNA are forms of reconstructive surveillance. Other systems used to monitor and gather intelligence include satellites, internet site traffic (social media and forum sites), phone networks, biometrics, aerial drones, human intelligence, and postal interception.

Surveillance while sometimes invasive is a key method to gather intelligence to prevent crimes, protect people, and guard property of interest. Social media sites can provide a rich compilation of information for mapping and data mining. A group can determine from search information relationships concerning personal or professional interests, friendships, affiliations, wants, beliefs, motivations, thoughts, political ideology, history of behavior, and financial standings.

Other types of surveillance includes the use of identification (credentials), Radio Frequency Identification (RFID) and geolocation devices are used with animals, humans, vehicles, and products. The Global positioning System (GPS) can be used to track devices in real time, this includes human microchips. Tracking microchips use an integrated circuit device with an RFID transponder, this is typically encased in silicate glass. Microchips are used in various manners to control, monitor, and identify people, animals, and cargo.

Covert listening and video devices known as bugs are used to capture, record, and or transmit data. Technology to open microphones and cameras on your phone or computer are used to hack access for information collection.

Just as there are ways to capture information, there are ways to intercept access to such information via countersurveillance. Human countermeasures include evasion, avoiding risky locations and activities, being discreet, and using code words or signals. Always be situationally aware, learn how to blend in with those around you, learn how to disappear, have locations to hide, and use measures to conceal identity. The use of device detection countermeasures include electronic sweeping. Most bugs emit some form of electromagnetic radiation in the frequencies of radio waves. A bug sweeper is a receiver that detects active bug transmissions.

The use of privacy software is a commonly used form of countersurveillance. Privacy software helps to prevent or interrupt cyber intrusion such as spying and stealing of valuable information. Be mindful in how you protect personal information and electronic based assets.

A History Lesson

History gives us a look at how past people dealt with threats, and how gray man tactics were used overcome challenges. One such example was during the warring state of feudal Japan - starting at about 1185. This timeline of war and conflict lasted for 700 years and demanded strategies and tactics of unconventional warfare. This included guerrilla warfare, espionage, and stealth tactics. What was used was a martial arts called Ninjutsu or the modern term ninpō. Outside of Japan ninjutsu is commonly known as ninja. It's important to note that ninjutsu had its origins much earlier, possibly 600 or more years before feudal Japan. Ninjutsu was developed and refined during the classical and medieval Japanese periods. Ninjutsu was established as a collection of fundamental survivalist techniques that were different than what was being taught in other traditional martial arts. Outside of fighting skills, the practitioner was also trained in methods of gathering information and techniques of non-detection, avoidance, and misdirection. Ninjutsu trained in free running, disguise, escape, evasion, concealment, archery, and medicine. Covert operations resulting in espionage and assassinations were useful to warring factions during violent political turmoil.

Ninjutsu adopted "the eighteen disciplines" as an outline of foundational disciplines to teach from and master. These include the following:

#1 Bajutsu – horsemanship

#2 Bōjutsu – stick and staff techniques

#3 Bōryaku – tactics

#4 Chi-mon – geography

#5 Chōhō – espionage

#6 Hensōjutsu – disguise and impersonation

#7 Intonjutsu – escape and concealment

#8 Kayakujutsu – pyrotechnics

#9 Kenjutsu – sword techniques

#10 Kusarigamajutsu – chain-sickle techniques

#11 Naginatajutsu – polearm techniques

#12 Seishinteki kyōyō – spiritual refinement

#13 Shinobi-iri –stealth and infiltration

#14 Shurikenjutsu – throwing weapons techniques

#15 Sōjutsu – spear techniques

#16 Sui-ren – water training

#17 Taijutsu – unarmed combat

#18 Tenmon – meteorology

Some of the ninjutsu composite and articulated weapons (tools) include the following:

Kusarigama – kama linked to a weight, either by a long rope or chain.

Kyoketsu-shoge – hooked rope-dart, featuring a metal ring on the opposite end.

Bō, Jō, Tambō, and Hanbō - wooden pole in various lengths.

Kusari-fundo – a chain and weight weapon.

Kakute – rings resembling modern wedding bands with concealed and often poison-tipped spines, typically worn by a female ninja, and enabling ninja to quietly strangle enemies with the pointed ends against the neck and throat.

Shobo – a jabbing or piercing weapon, similar in shape to kubaton and yawara, but often featuring a center grip ring.

Shuriken – various small hand-held weapons including throwing stars, darts and blades that could be used to stab, slash or throw.

Kubaton – a hand stick used mainly for pressure points, subduing, and forced pain compliance of opponents.

Tekko – an early version of brass knuckles.

Tessen – a folding fan with an iron frame. It could be used to club or slash the enemy.

Jitte – a weapon similar to the sai. A traditional piercing melee weapon of a pointed prong shaped metal baton containing two curved prongs projecting from the handle.

Kunai – a multi-purpose tool which can be used for farming in turning up crops or hand shoveling. In martial arts it's used to gouge holes in walls, as a climbing aid, and a throwing weapon.

Shikoro – was a carpenter tool used by the ninja for opening doors, gates, stabbing, slashing or cutting.

Fukiya – a Japanese blowgun, typically firing poison darts.

Makibishi – a type of caltrop or spiked metal device thrown on the ground to impede wheeled vehicles or cavalry horses.

Yumi and Ya – traditional Japanese bow and arrow.

Bo-hiya – a fire arrow.

Tekagi-shuko and Neko-te – hand claw weapons.

Chakram – disk-like projectiles used as throwing weapons or in hand-to-hand combat.

Yari – traditional Japanese spear similar to the naginata.

Nagamaki – pole arm with roughly equal-length blade and handle.

Naginata – traditional Japanese pole-arm used by women and samurai.

Katana – a long curved and single-edged sword, commonly used by ninja who disguised themselves as samurai.

Wakizashi – a short sword that can be hidden on the ninja's body, also used as a backup weapon.

Ninjatō – an edged weapon used by ninja as a sword.

Tantō – a dagger.

Kaiken – similar to the tantō.

Bokken – a traditional wooden sword used in Japanese martial arts, typically modeled off of katanas.

Shinai – a bamboo sword used in kendō. This Japanese martial art of swordsmanship also incorporates protective armor and was used to simulate combat.

Kaginawa – a grappling hook used for climbing and a makeshift gaff hook weapon.

Shinobi shōzoku – the reputed ninja clothing.

Ono – Japanese axe and hatchet.

Ninjutsu is mindful of not telegraphing movement and thus not advertising intention. The ninja is calm and quiet but strikes with precision and the element of surprise. The ninja allows the opponent(s) to become overly confident, then uses this to expose and exploit weakness.

Efficient Living

A gray man should be as independent as possible. This means dependency on society should be avoided and replaced with proactive self-sustaining behavior. Reflect on that which influences you. Work to broaden your circle of influence and address issues before they become problems.

Begin with the end in mind – look at the bigger picture. Consider working from the desired outcome of a goal to expose solutions and develop strategy. This is called reverse engineering, it allows you to trek from the desired end goal to your present problem solving challenges. But before you make a plan - specifically know what you want. The more detailed the better.

Put first things first – know your priorities. Work with others when a project or goal is larger than your resources. This use of interdependence is smart and beneficial to not just you but to others with the same objective.

Think win-win. The more you obsess about something the more energy you put into it to make it happen.

Value and respect others – this allows for mutual benefits for multiple parties concerning solution development and agreement.

Seek first to understand – then to be understood. Use empathy and listening skills to enhance understanding. Positive influence creates an atmosphere of caring and results in more dynamic problem solving. Personal credibility, empathy, emotional trust, and logic allows you to understand and be understood.

Synergize – combine the strengths of people to create a force and resource larger than yourself to solve grander goals. Continuously improve in your personal and interpersonal spheres of influence. The gray man seeks to stay balanced by being grounded and practicing effective means to renew resources, energy, and health. Every person is different so know what works best for you. Pay attention to your conscious, body, and emotions to gauge your state and to be able to influence it for personal growth.

Lastly, inspire others – the more you do for another the better off we all are.

The following are productivity tips. Productivity is a major trait of the gray man, you must be effective in making things happen or risk suffering.

Prioritize by doing first what matters. For many this may call for a reduction of things you set out to do each day. An overwhelming extensive to do list tends to work against productivity, keep your daily list simple and practical.

Take more breaks – eat a snack to replace burnt glycogen, take a walk to remove yourself from an environment and stimulate other parts of the brain, and consider taking 10 to 20 minute power naps to rejuvenate and reset your focus and drive. A popular way to recharge is by listening to your favorite music. Find ways to recharge in any environment.

Use the 80/20 rule – this states approximately 20% of what you do produces 80% of your results. Test it out in real life and see for yourself. What are the things you do that get the most results? Eliminate the things that don't matter, that waste time, and that can be automated or outsourced. The more you leverage your time the more productive you can be.

Get up early – make time for yourself. This may translate into a form of meditation, prayer, or exercise. Know what is effective and be consistent. Get your largest challenges done by lunch. Doing your principal and most difficult work first frees you from more menial work later. Set a flow of accomplishments that builds on itself. Addressing your most important work early also takes advantage of your rested state - this provides needed focus and clarity. Focus and clarity are major contributors to efficiency.

Cut out email and social media notifications – reduce clutter to make room for things you want to do with your limited time. Don't be held captive to what others do and say.

Assign a time to do certain tasks – create a schedule or system that efficiently manages your time. Set time slots to check phone calls, email, social media, and to look up news. If you like to surf the web be sure to create time for that as well.

Confront laziness – idleness is a large and common factor from which yields negative results. Laziness and productivity repel each other.

Stop multitasking- the more you multitask the lower your efficiency and concentration. Distraction is not your friend. Do one thing at a time for safer efficient results. Protect your attention span to maximize focus and allow for better problem solving opportunities.

Make plans for the next day - make every day count by having a plan. Some days your plan might be to simply relax, but by knowing ahead of time you can maximize your purpose.

Take care of your health – eat well, get enough sleep, and manage your stress efficiently. The healthier you are the more capable you can be.

Plan meals for the week – use a meal plan to maximize your time and energy. Prepare meals in advance to be used at a later date. Reducing time devoted to food prep will expand your time allotment for productivity.

Create a wardrobe lineup for the week - organize clothing in your drawers and closet so that each outfit is next in line for use. Clothing management saves time and reduces anxiety in those who worry about these matters.

Delegate work when possible - time is a finite resource, allow others to help you reach your goals. Be comfortable in saying no to those who waste your time, take advantage of you, and disrespect your friendship. Don't be a slave to other people's work. When delegating work to others always be sincere, appreciative, respectful, and rewarding. Rewards may come in the form of cash, gift cards, services, or other desirable outcomes.

Simplify life – declutter the spaces in your life where stuff interferes with emotional wellbeing. Know your stressors and remove or minimize from your life. Know what provides you peace, use that when needed.

Leave emotional baggage where it is - don't feel tempted to carry it throughout your life. Let every day be a new beginning. Leave yesterday's mistakes, disappointments, losses, and embarrassments in the past. Today is a new day and the start of a new life. The past is history while the future is full of potential and mystery.

Economical Gray Man

Those on a budget know the realities, but with simple planning and forethought most can find opportunities to acquire what is needed. Essentials should be the first priority, what do you need to function efficiently? Research all categories and products thoroughly. Identify high quality and high value products. Stay away from new to the market gear that is untested, gimmicky, and blatant knockoffs. Delay purchases until you are confident that you have identified the right gear at the right price.

The following are examples of various types of gear and factors to consider when putting together an everyday carry system. For simplicity here's a look at lights, blades, multitools, pocket organizers, and lighters:

Lights – size, weight, light output, light modes, color of light, beam type, battery type, run times, moisture resistance, impact resistance, type of bezel, heat management technology, reverse polarity protection, anti-roll design, grip texturing, retention options, fit & finish, construction materials, purpose of use, price, level of value, warranty, accessories, anti-reflective lens coating, anodized finish, lanyard hole, momentary on, position of controls, tail stand capability, overall comfort, ease of use, how it compares to similar models, and does it meet your needs?

Blades – size, weight, color, design, grind, blade steel, heat treat, handle material, locking action, purpose of use, fit & finish, retention options, accessories, price, warranty, rust resistance, impact resistance, level of value, ease of use, comfort in hand, how it compares to similar models, and does it meet your needs?

Multitools – size, weight, color, tool selection, purpose of use, construction materials, action of tool implements, design, fit & finish, retention options, accessories, price, level of value, warranty, rust resistance, durability, replaceability of tools, ease of use, comfort in use, how it compares to similar models, and does it meet your needs?

Pocket organizers – size, weight, color, number of compartments, organizational potential, moisture resistance, durability, fit & finish, purpose, how it compares to similar models, price, level of value, warranty, which size pockets will it fit into, what do you plan on storing, construction materials, zippers, thread type, fabric type, ease of use, comfort in pocket, does it meet your needs?

Lighters – size, weight, color, fuel type, fuel reserve capacity, ignition mechanism, carryability, ease of use, level of value, price, comfort in hand, durability, product history, safety features, moisture resistance, impact resistance, overall quality, purpose, warranty, how it compared to similar models, functionality of design, and does it meet your needs?

Consider rechargeable devices over non rechargeable ones, this will save you money over time. To streamline your gear, use devices that share the same batteries, chargers, and accessories when possible.

Warranties make a difference. Use only reputable companies that have a history of backing their products.

Keep gear clean and maintained. A maintained piece of gear will function more efficiently, be more reliable, and last longer.

Don't be tempted to upgrade gear if the need is not present. Just because others are buying the newest version does not mean that it's justifiable for you to do the same. Use what works – looks are not everything.

Use yard sales, flea markets, and trading with friends to save money over buying new.

Don't sell yourself on supplies that won't be used. Just because the price is right doesn't mean that the purchase would benefit you.

Take advantage of sales, clearances, and specials on needed items. There's no need to pay full price.

Repurpose gear you already own. This could be as simple and reusing a handle on a mop or using spare lumber to build a project.

Make your gear when possible, otherwise ask a friend to make it for you.

Use timing to secure a deal. Certain opportunities require immediate action to acquire supplies at deeply discounted pricing. By having money set aside for buying opportunities you can take advantage of said deal. Some deals are advertised in advance, this makes it easier to prepare for.

Memberships can be a source of discounted merchandise. Shop wisely though, not all member only retailers are providing deep discounts.

Exclusive promotions and discounted pre-orders may provide an opportunity to secure gear more affordably. Always price compare to gauge the value of a deal.

Avoid fads and use tried and true gear. Trying to save a few bucks on an inferior product will eventually become a regretful purchase.

Shop during the week for better selection and avoid the weekend traffic. It's not uncommon for stores to also provide the deepest discounts during the week.

Order online to save time and fuel. You can order in the comfort of your home and not have to deal with crowds and traffic. Many online retailers provide free shipping and deeper discounts than in brick and mortar stores.

Priority Gear Exercise

What gear benefits you the most? What are the essentials – the priority items? Use this mental exercise to develop a core gear list. Use mental exercises like this to solve other objectives.

With all things considered what would your priority gear / supply list look like? You can limit the number of items to make it a challenge or to meet a certain requirement.

Here are my top picks for most useful gear, use these examples to compare to your own and to help brainstorm:

100% Wool U.S. Military Issued Blanket

2 Quart Stainless Steel Ozark Trail Cooking Pot

200'of Gladding Mil Spec 550 type III Parachute Cord

3M Corded Reusable Earplugs

40 Ounce Wide Mouth Stainless Steel Klean Kanteen Water Bottle and Toaks 550 Milliliter Titanium Nesting Cup

5.11 Tactical COVRT 18 Backpack

AmazonBasics 8'x10' Rip-Stop Fabric Camping Tarp

Anker 10,000 mAh Power Pack / Battery Bank

Anker 21 Watt USB Solar Charger

Bahco Laplander Folding Hand Saw

Bic Lighter & Light My Fire Swedish Firesteel 2.0 Army

Cellular Phone + Spare Battery, Charger, & Protective Case

Collapsible Fishing Pole, Tackle, Gill Net, Snares, and Traps

Covacure Hammock with Bug Netting

Custom Built First Aid and Trauma Kit / IFAK Built on a Condor Rip-Away EMT Pouch

Emberlit FireAnt Titanium Ultralight Backpacking Stove

Frogg Toggs Rain Suit and Poncho

Giant ATX 27.5 2 Off Road Trail / Mountain Bicycle

Glock 26 + 2 Spare Loaded Magpul PMAG 12 GL9 Magazines and Concealment Holster

Kelty Salida Camping and Backpacking Tent

Kelty Tuck Ex 0 ThermaPro Sleeping Bag

Lansky Blademedic Knife & Tool Sharpener

Leatherman Rebar or Surge Multitool

Leupold Rogue Compact Porro Prism 10x25mm Binocular

Marksman #3040 Slingshot with Pathfinder Pocket Hunter Adaptor (30 lbs. at 28" draw) or Chief AJ's HFX Slingshot

Maxpedition Fatty Pocket Organizer in Foliage Green

Pyramex Highlander or 3M Virtua CCS Protective Eyewear

Roll of Gorilla Tape

Rothco Genuine GI Earplugs

Rothco Sniper Veil, Shemagh, and Bandana

Ruger 10/22 Stainless Steel Takedown Rifle + Aftermarket Stock, Sound Suppressor, Red Dot Sights, and 2 Spare Loaded 25 Round BX-25 Magazines

SAS Survival Guide by John 'Lofty' Wiseman (I like his survival information but not his politics)

Sawyer MINI Water Filter

SGE 400 NBC Gas Mask

SOL Rescue Flash or UST StarFlash Multi-tool Signal Mirror

Spyderco Delica 4 (fine edge) & Spyderco Salt 2 (serrated) Folding Blades

Stainless Steel Mora Garberg, Mora Companion or Mora Kansbol

Storm Safety Whistle

Local Topographic Maps, Suunto MC-2 Compass and SealLine Map Case

Tru-Spec Hot Weather Type II 65% Polyester 35% Cotton Boonie Hat

U.S. GI Issued Boots

U.S. Military Issued Folding Shovel / E-Tool

USB Rechargeable AM/FM/SW TIVDIO V-115 Portable Radio/Recorder/Player

Wet Wipes, Dental Floss, Toothbrush, Toothpaste, Hand Sanitizer, Microfiber Wash Cloth, Toilet Paper and Bar of Soap

WowTac A1S Flashlight, WowTac A2S Headlamp or Streamlight PolyTac X Flashlight (all lights are USB rechargeable)

Additional Gray Man Quotes

"I am an invisible man. I am a man of substance, of flesh and bone, fiber and liquids – and I might even be said to possess a mind. I am invisible, understand, simply because people refuse to see me." – Ralph Ellison

"I'm interested in the murky areas where there are no clear answers – or sometimes multiple answers. It's here that I try to imagine patterns or codes to make sense of the unknowns that keep us up at night. I'm also interested in the invisible space between people in communication, the space guided by translation and misinterpretation." – Taryn Simon

"One of the most pervasive mistakes is to believe that our visual system gives a faithful representation of what is "out there" in the same way that a movie camera would." – David Eagleman

"The lone, ordinary person, existing incognito within the system has tremendous power in a revolution." – Bryant McGill

"…we are not conscious of most things until we ask ourselves questions about them" – David Eagleman

"People don't want to hear the truth because they don't want their illusions destroyed." – Friedrich Nietzsche

"seeing has little to do with your eyes." – David Eagleman

"Vision is the art of seeing what is invisible to others." – Jonathan Swift

"awareness of your surroundings occurs only when sensory inputs violate expectations. When the world is successfully predicted away, awareness is not needed because the brain is doing its job well." – David Eagleman

"Rarely have I witnessed assumptions turn into facts." – Sonya Teclai

"Vision is active, not passive. There is more than one way for the visual system to interpret the stimulus, and so it flips back and forth between the possibilities." – David Eagleman

"The more often we see the things around us – even the beautiful and wonderful things – the more they become invisible to us. That is why we often take for granted the beauty of this world: the flowers, the trees, the birds, the clouds – even those we love. Because we see things so often, we see them less and less." – Joseph B. Wirthlin

"The sky is filled with stars, invisible by day." – Henry Wadsworth Longfellow

"Man, when I'm riding with the helmet on, I'm invisible. And people just deal with me as the guy on the bike… it gives you a chance to read'em." – Brad Pitt

"The true mystery of the world is the visible, not the invisible." – Oscar Wilde

"The battles that count aren't the ones for gold medals. The struggles within yourself – the invisible, inevitable battles inside all of us – that's where it's at." – Jesse Owens

"Bridges are perhaps the most invisible form of public architecture." – Bruce Jackson

"Ninety-nine percent of who you are is invisible and untouchable." – R. Buckminster Fuller

"When our spelling is perfect, it's invisible. But when it's flawed, it prompts strong negative associations." – Marilyn vos Savant

"Behind the ostensible government sits enthroned an invisible government owing no allegiance and acknowledging no responsibility to the people." – Theodore Roosevelt

"The real rulers in Washington are invisible, and exercise power from behind the scenes." – Felix Frankfurter

"You can't assume any place you go is private because the means of surveillance are becoming so affordable and so invisible." – Howard Rheingold

"All that stuff about James bond, that's Hollywood. You don't want anyone standing out in the intelligence business. You want someone nondescript. The ideal spy is 5-foot-6 and kind of dumpy." – Bob Ayers

"I always think my face is quite nondescript – it sort of fits in to any period. It's not really distinct enough for you to remember me from something." – Kimberley Nixon

"Our mobile phones have become the greatest spy on the planet." – John McAfee

"You can't be a real spy and have everyone in the world know who you are and what your drink is. That's just hysterically funny." – Roger Moore

"I've always wanted to play a spy, because it is the ultimate acting exercise. You are never what you seem." – Benedict Cumberbatch

"Imagine a 'Mission: Impossible'-style spy or infiltration mission into the core, the very heart of the Empire's military-industrial complex, the most secure facility in the Empire. You have a small band of experts with complementary skills who, together, are able to do these amazing things." – John Knoll

Summary

Being gray is going unnoticed – unassuming. This takes time to develop so be patient with yourself as you develop these new skills. Unpretentious interactions with others will help you blend in and get overlooked. Minimize any contrast between the environment and what you add to it. The more you contrast the more attention from others you will receive. People become more aware of that which is different from the environmental baseline. Demonstrate and practice gray man skills in an inconspicuous manner. Always be inquisitive and look at the world with fresh eyes - never stop learning. Stay in a state of relaxed alertness, awareness of your surroundings helps solve problems and prevent negative outcomes.

In closing I want to mention an important overlooked aspect of being gray, and that is of stillness. The quiet within us is a resource worthy of cultivation. Spend time in your stillness and discover the many benefits it holds. Stillness enhances focus, extinguishes fear, and provides a state of peak performance. This inner state helps to develop higher levels of self-mastery in all we do. The development of inner strength enhances the state of grayness.

Be the unseen, the sound of silent shadows.

Gray Man Gear Checklists

Gray Man Everyday Carry

__ Bandana / handkerchief

__ Blade

__ Cell phone

__ Firestarter

__ Food

__ Hat

__ Keys / key accessories

__ Lethal self-defense tools

__ Light

__ Lip balm

__ Multitool

__ Non-lethal self-defense tools

__ Note pad

__ Pocket first aid kit

__ Pocket organizer

__ Power pack

__ Storage drives / thumb drives

__ Sunglasses

__ Wallet

__ Watch

__ Writing tools

Gray Man Everyday Carry Bag

__ 2-way radio

__ Bandana / shemagh

__ Chalk

__ Change of clothing

__ Chargers / solar chargers

__ Compact emergency radio

__ Compass

__ Cordage

__ Duct tape

__ Ear protection

__ Eye protection

__ Firearm accessories / spare ammunition

__ Firestarter

__ First aid / trauma kit

__ Fixed blade survival knife

__ Folding knife

__ Gloves

__ GPS

__ Headlamp

__ Laptop / tablet or other electronics

__ Lightweight tarp

__ Maps

__ Multitool

__ Note pad

__ Pepper spray / collapsible baton

__ Rain gear

__ Ready to eat foods

__ Sniper veil

__ Spare batteries / battery bank

__ Spare cell phone

__ Tinder

__ Water / water bottle

__ Water filter

__ Writing tools

Gray Man Survival Kit

__ Backpack – durable / lightweight / spacious / well organized

__ Cordage – parachute cord / bank line

__ Cutting tools – fixed blade survival knife / hand saw / collapsible bow saw / camp ax / hatchet

__ Fire – firestarters / tinder / water proof container

__ Food – lightweight nutrient dense options

__ Information – compact survival reference / portable emergency NOAA / AM / FM / Shortwave radio

__ Lighting – flashlight / headlamp / chemlights / candles / mini lanterns

__ Medical – First aid / trauma kit

__ Navigation – compass / GPS / maps / trail markers / ranger beads

__ Protection – non lethal / lethal options

__ Repair – duct tape / zip ties / adhesives / sewing kit

__ Resources – identification / cash / bank – insurance – land title documents

__ Shelter – tent / tarp / hammock

__ Signaling – whistle / signal mirror / flare / cell phone / transponder

__ Specialized tools – lock picks / listening devices / bug detectors

__ Trade & barter – batteries / tape / wire / cordage / tobacco products / fishing hooks

__ Water – filter / container

Gray Man Specialized Gear

__ Balaclava face mask

__ Binoculars

__ Body armor - blunt force/trauma soft body armor

__ Bug detector /RF scanner

__ Collapsible / folding carbine

__ Concealed carry firearm and accessories

__ Concealed cutting tools – neck, ankle, inside waistband blades

__ Covert backpacks and sling packs

__ Covert tactical clothing

__ Dyneema puncture resistant gloves

__ Enhanced sound detection gear

__ Face paint

__ IFAK – individual first aid kit / trauma kit

__ Impact resistant eyewear

__ Low output red & blue lights

__ Night vision

__ Radio scanner

__ Sniper veil

__ Thermal optics

__ Voice Scrambler

__ Wig & other disguises

Skill Checklist

__ Camouflage

__ Coded communications

__ Cooking

__ Fire making

__ Gear repair

__ Hunting / trapping / fishing / foraging

__ Information gathering

__ Knife sharpening

__ Knot making

__ Lock picking

__ Medical

__ Navigation

__ Self defense

__ Sewing

__ Shelter building

__ Signaling

__ Stealth Camping

__ Tool making

__ Torch making

__ Water purification

Notes

<u>Notes</u>

<u>Notes</u>

www.ingramcontent.com/pod-product-compliance
Lightning Source LLC
Chambersburg PA
CBHW061404250726
48657CB00004B/1644